June Draw...

SOUL RETRIEVAL

SOUL RETRIEVAL

MENDING THE FRAGMENTED SELF

SANDRA INGERMAN

HarperSanFrancisco
A Division of HarperCollins*Publishers*

The shamanic way of healing using soul retrieval presented in this book should not be considered an exclusive method of confronting psychological and/or medical problems. It should be viewed as an adjunct to orthodox medical or psychological treatments.

Harper San Francisco and the author, in association with the Rainforest Action Network, will facilitate the planting of two trees for every one tree used in the manufacture of this book.

Illustrations by Jaye Oliver

The copyright page continues on page 223, following the index.

Library of Congress Cataloging-in-Publication Data

Ingerman, Sandra.
    Soul Retrieval : mending the fragmented self / Sandra Ingerman.
    —1st ed.
    p. cm.
    Includes bibliographic references and index.
    ISBN 0–06–250406–1
    1. Spiritual healing   2. Shamanism   3. Soul   I. Title.
BL65.M4145   1991   90–56447
615.8'52—dc20   CIP

93 94 95 ❖ RRD(H)   10 9 8 7

To my brother, Joseph, and to my parents, Aaron and Lee.

This book is a gift from the moon to the sun.

CONTENTS

FOREWORD

With the current revival of shamanism and shamanic healing, we are at last beginning to recognize the spiritual and psychological value of much that our ancestors knew. Indeed, we are
learning not only to respect this great storehouse of ancient human knowledge but also to understand its potential importance
to our own well-being and health.

We of the "civilized" world often tend to dismiss the strange
beliefs of tribal peoples as superstitions or prehistoric curiosities
with no relevance to our own lives. Certainly the widespread tribal belief in "soul loss" as a major factor in illness has typically fall-
en into this category. Even the least ethnocentric anthropologists
have been hard put to view this concept as anything more than
an archaic cultural artifact. This book by Sandra Ingerman over-
turns such stereotypes about soul loss and shows that the ancient
shamanic methods for treating soul loss have urgent applicability
to the traumas of contemporary life, including the consequences
of incest and other forms of childhood abuse.

This is a dramatic case of a supposedly "superstitious" and
"primitive" belief system being directly relevant to modern life. I
remember the excitement in Sandra Ingerman's voice when she
telephoned me several years ago to share her discovery that
shamanic soul retrieval work was yielding remarkable healing results for her women clients who, as children, had experienced sexual abuse. Such a discovery would not surprise tribal shamans, of
course, who have long used soul retrieval as a healing technique

for all kinds of traumas, even the most subtle ones. But for Sandra Ingerman and myself, it was another confirmation of the great importance of reviving and applying the time-tested healing methods of the shaman to our health problems today. It was again clear to us that shamanic healing methods worked at the most profound levels imaginable, with such deep impact that cultural differences were virtually irrelevant.

In the eleven years I have known her, Sandra Ingerman has moved from being one of my students of shamanic practice to being an outstanding shaman, an esteemed colleague, and a treasured friend. Beyond that, she is an inspiring teacher, as can be attested by her many students. What you read here by her, you can trust, for she exemplifies the highest standards of ethics and practical knowledge in contemporary shamanism and shamanic healing. If you feel, as most people do, that you have lost portions of your own soul in the trials and traumas of life, pay careful attention to what she says. If you wish to go further and try the method for yourself, I strongly recommend training with her in the technique firsthand. I can suggest no better teacher for helping one learn how to become spiritually whole again.

Michael Harner
Norwalk, Connecticut
December 1990

ACKNOWLEDGMENTS

There are so many people whom I want to acknowledge and thank. I received countless phone calls and letters from friends, students, and clients, always asking how the book was going, encouraging me with their words of support, constantly reminding me how important it was to share this work with others, and thanking me for introducing soul retrieval into their lives. Their words gave me the courage and energy to continue—to them there is no way to adequately express my gratitude.

I am grateful to Dot Dusek for giving me the inspiration to write. I also want to thank those who helped in the editing process. Mary Lois Sennewald worked in the beginning phase of the book. Craig Comstock continued working as a "literary soul retriever," helping me find the essence of the book and teaching me about animating my writing. Craig also was invaluable in writing the book proposal. And Cynthia Bechtel, who did the editing after the book proposal was done, showed me that I was a writer and didn't need as much help as I thought I did. Cynthia's honoring of my writing inspired my creativity—to her I am most grateful.

Christina Crawford supported me in both seen and unseen ways. She helped me journey on the book; she was a constant support both to me and to the book and generously helped me research the literature.

Jaye Oliver illustrated the book, helping me bring some of the territories of nonordinary reality into visual form.

I thank Polly Rose for her assistance in typing the manuscript and being patient with all my deadlines.

My agent Katinka Matson, my editor Barbara Moulton, and editorial assistant Barbara Archer at Harper San Francisco introduced me to the publishing world in a very peaceful, friendly, and gracious way. Barbara Moulton made me feel welcome at Harper.

And then there were those close to home who provided me with loving care: my parents, Aaron and Lee Ingerman; Marla, Robert, Johanna, and Alex Becker Black, the family I lived with and who cared for me during the two years I spent writing this book; and Easy Hill, my partner, for his calm presence and his unconditional love and understanding.

Some of those who helped me with the actual soul retrieval work are: Michael Harner, who has been a wonderful teacher and friend over the last eleven years; Sharon Bergeron, MFCC, who so generously consulted with me on the psychological effects of incest to prepare me for my work with incest survivors; and all my students, who contributed to the re-pioneering of this wonderful work.

I also want to acknowledge the people who were willing to share so generously their personal letters used in this book as well as those who wrote and shared their poetry with us. The poets are Ellen Jaffe Bitz, Ailo Gaup, Diana Rowan, and Stephen Van Buren.

I give a very special thanks to my power animals and teachers in nonordinary reality who taught me, supported me, and worked in partnership with me to be able to present *Soul Retrieval* to you.

SOUL RETRIEVAL

INTRODUCTION

Soul loss is a spiritual illness that causes emotional and physical disease. Who takes care of our spirit when it gets sick? We have doctors for the body, for the mind, and for the heart, but what do we do when our spirit is ailing? This book speaks to the issue of spirit and the healing of spiritual matters. Around the world and across many cultures, a person who deals with the spiritual aspect of illness is a shaman. A shaman diagnoses and treats illnesses, divines information, communicates and interacts with the spirit world, and occasionally acts as a psychopomp, that is, a person who helps souls cross over to the other world.

Mircea Eliade, author of *Shamanism: Archaic Techniques of Ecstasy,* describes a shaman as a person who makes a journey in an altered state of consciousness outside time and space.[1] The word *shaman,* which comes from the Tungus tribe in Siberia, refers equally to women and men. Through journeys, a shaman retrieves aid and information to help a patient, family, friends, or community.

Generally, a shaman uses percussion or, less frequently, psychoactive drugs as a means to enter into an altered state. Anthropologists trace this practice back tens of thousands of years. Michael Harner, anthropologist and author of *The Way of the Shaman,* has investigated shamanism in cultures all over the world. Like Eliade, he found that a shaman is particularly distinguished from other healers by the use of the journey.[2] Evidence of shamanic journeys is found in Siberia, Lapland, parts of Asia, Africa, Australia, and native North and South America.

This book will discuss one common cause of illness—soul loss. The emphasis here will be on using this classical diagnosis and ancient system to treat modern-day problems that come from a variety of traumas we all bear in life.

In the chapters that follow I will explain shamanism and soul loss to you, drawing from classical resources, my own teaching and practice, and case studies on the effects of this work. (The individuals who appear in the case studies are composites created from real situations and do not represent specific individuals.)

The concepts I will talk about may be very hard to understand from a rational, logical place. In our society and our culture, we tend to support left-brain functions. The left brain is the logical and rational part of ourselves, and it is wonderful (for example, it facilitated your going out and buying this book). But as we learn more and more in the evolution of our consciousness, we discover that reality is not as logical as we may have supposed it to be. There is more to be "seen" than what can be seen literally by the human eye.

Many of us embark upon a spiritual path to expand our awareness and wake up abilities that have gone dormant, to experience and perceive more of life than we are able to by drawing on logic alone. In order to do this we use our right-brain functions. We must open to our intuition. We must use our senses to perceive reality in a different way. We must see, hear, feel, and smell from a different place inside ourselves. And when we learn to expand all our senses, we can then step into the world of the shaman.

But new belief systems are sometimes hard to deal with. Using the intuitive part of ourselves is just not accepted in our society. We've developed such a structured system that to leave it is seen as dangerous. We've lost our imagination. How can we envision a healthy planet, or a healthy body, or success, if we can't imagine or envision what we want?

Children are constantly aware of other realities. But a different belief system is forced upon all of us at a very early age. Do you remember as a child being told to stop talking to your imaginary friends? Or to stop daydreaming? We were born understanding hidden realities. We naturally knew the way of the shaman, but we had to unlearn the path as we became socialized. Many of us are turning back to that way.

When people begin to journey to nonordinary reality, often they wonder, "Am I making this up?" Society as it is today would respond yes. A shaman would say, "Did you see it, or hear it, or feel it, or smell it?" If one answers yes, a shaman's reply would be, "Well, what's wrong with you that you think you're making it up?"

These are two opposing answers to the question of whether nonordinary reality is "real." This question challenges not only the ego but also all that we hear from our parents, teachers, government, and often religious leaders, as well as from scientists. When all these figures of authority tell us what the nature of reality is, it establishes a strong belief system that I have no intention of fighting.

As you read this book and wonder whether or not what I am talking about is "real," I ask you not to enter into a battle between the right brain and left brain. Simply read the material and experience it. After eleven years of working with the shamanic journey I know nonordinary reality is real. But I don't intend to convince you of that. For me, the big questions are these: Does the information that comes from a shamanic journey work? Does this information make positive changes in a person's life? If so, who cares if we are making it up?

Consider my journeys however you need to. When I share my experiences with my clients I always say, "I'm going to tell you what I saw." The individual needs to decide if the information is metaphorical or literal. One might view the journeys as a waking dream or as information coming from the unconscious in symbolic representation. Or one might think of nonordinary reality as a world parallel to ours.

This book is written for all the children of the world, and that means each and every person who reads it. Right now we face a crucial struggle on this planet. How do we grow up and use our powers of judgment and insight to be responsible for all forms of life? How can we contact and integrate the child that lives inside each of us—that child who has the power of creative imagination to envision what we can create?

The basis of this book is the concept of soul loss—losing crucial parts of ourselves that provide us with life and vitality. These parts get lost through trauma, and who has suffered the most trauma but the children who live inside us? Here I provide a look at soul retrieval, an ancient technique in shamanism that can help bring the children "home." This is only the beginning of our work, however, for bringing the children home is ultimately not very hard. The difficult and exciting work is the partnership between child and adult. In this process we take the life and light of the child, with its curiosity and imagination, and allow it to see for us adults and tell us what is true. Then the adult can act on the child's visions to bring them to fruition and yet use mature discretion in knowing the appropriate timing—the union of opposite but complementary modes of existence.

When I first took a shamanic journey to talk to my teacher in nonordinary reality about writing this book, all she would say to me was, "Write, and write from your heart." Every morning before I started to write, I would repeat the journey with the hope that I would get some little tidbit of information. I would make the rounds to my power animal and my teacher, and they both were firm in their message.

So I wrote. I wrote three chapters, and at that point I decided to journey again and see whether my teacher or power animal would be willing to comment on the work I had done so far. My teacher was waiting for me when I reached her home in the Upper World, and she said that I was moving in the wrong direction. She said that the book as I had it set up initially would frighten people; it would make them feel that if they did not have a soul retrieval, they would never lead a happy life. She said this book must be a healing for every person who reads it, whether or not they ever decide to have a soul retrieval.

To make reading the book more experiential, most chapters will have one or more exercises intended to bring you closer to the world of spirit in a gentle and safe way. If any of the information or stories included here evoke a part of your own internal child that is afraid, sad, or angry, turn to the exercise in chapter 11 that helps you deal with these feelings.

My purpose in writing *Soul Retrieval* is to offer a new way of thinking about the cause of illness, one that has been acknowledged for thousands of years but is not being recognized by traditional schools of physical and psychological healing. I also offer some tools to you who choose to enter into harmony with the universe and move forward in your own soul's journey.

PART I

THE SOUL AND SOUL LOSS

CHAPTER 1

SOUL LOSS

For what is a man profited, if he shall
gain the whole world, and lose
his own soul?
—Jesus Christ

To get the most out of this book I feel it is important for you to go to a place very deep inside yourself, a place where you can distinguish essential truth from "mind chatter." To do this, I would like you to try a simple exercise I have used for years to help clients discover the difference between intuition and mind interference.[1]

Begin by sitting comfortably in a chair. Close your eyes, take four deep breaths, and try to relax as fully as you can. Now think about something you love, something very simple, like a color, a flower, a food. Tell yourself, "I love . . ." Repeat it. Just experience in your body what it feels like when you tell yourself a truth. Now get up and do something for a few minutes. If you're at home, do something around the house. If you're out, walk around for a few minutes. Then come back and sit down and close your eyes. Take four more deep breaths. And now tell yourself a lie. Say to yourself, "I hate . . ."(the same thing you just said you loved). Repeat the phrase "I hate . . ." and try to experience what your body does when it hears a lie.

When I hear a lie, a red flag pops up in my solar plexus. When I'm listening to someone or reading, I can know if I'm hearing an essential truth by noticing whether or not the red flag comes up. If I'm trying to make a decision and my mind won't stop interfering in my process with its chatter, I say to myself what I'm getting ready to do and then I watch for the red flag. If it doesn't come up, I move forward, even if my mind is kicking and screaming all the way.

Other people report with this exercise that with a truth a warm sensation floods the body, or goose bumps or tingling sensations are felt throughout the body; a general peace may overcome them, or their heart may feel good. With a lie, a tightness occurs in the chest or solar plexus, or a particular color may come to mind, or there may be some feeling of distress in the body.

In this book I will be speaking to a space very deep inside you. I will be sparking your essence to wake up and come alive. The conscious mind might not always understand what I'm trying to say. And sometimes I will even try to bypass the mind so that your own inner knowing can participate in your healing process.

Throughout your reading, watch for the kinesthetic signs or body sensations that will give you a way for your deeper sense to say yes and continue. Whether or not you ever actually receive a soul retrieval, this book will provide you with a healing. It will teach you how we lose our vitality and essence, how we remain fragmented, and how we can make a conscious decision to move toward a more fulfilling life.

We all spend a tremendous amount of psychic energy looking for lost parts of ourselves. We do this unconsciously, and we do this in many different ways—generating dreams and daydreams, experimenting with numerous spiritual paths, creating relationships that mirror back to us our missing parts.

Many of us today don't feel totally whole, don't feel as if we are all here. Few of us live as fully as we could. When we become aware of this, we want to recover the intensity of life, and the intimacy, that we once enjoyed or of which we hold an image. We want to come home more fully to ourselves and to the people we love.

A technique exists for dealing with this common human predicament, but this technique has been almost entirely forgotten in modern society. For tens of thousands of years a practice known as shamanism has brought healing to people in many cultures around the world. According to the shamanic perspective, one of the major causes of illness is soul loss.

The word *soul* has taken on many meanings. Here I use it simply to mean our vital essence, or as the *Oxford English Dictionary* (second edition) says, "the principle of life, commonly regarded as an entity distinct from the body; the spiritual parts in contrast to the purely physical." According to this authority, our language also regards the soul as the seat of the emotions, feelings, or sentiments.

Keeping this image of soul in mind, we can ask what causes the loss of this vital essence. In ancient times, loss of this kind was attributed to the soul being frightened away, or straying, or being stolen. Today we often find soul loss is a result of such traumas as incest, abuse, loss of a loved one, surgery, accident, illness, miscarriage, abortion, the stress of combat, or addiction.

The basic premise is that whenever we experience trauma, a part of our vital essence separates from us in order to survive the experience by escaping the full impact of the pain. What constitutes trauma varies from one individual to another. Soul loss can be caused by whatever a person experiences as traumatic, even if another person would not experience it as such.

In modern times, psychology has provided our primary model for addressing the painful sense of incompleteness and disconnection that many of us experience. We may spend years in therapy or self-help groups trying to uncover traumas and to become whole. I hold a master's degree in counseling psychology and have employed many of its methods, but experience has shown me that psychotherapy works only on the parts of us that are "home."

If a part of our vital essence has fled, how can we bring it back? Seeking an answer to this question, I turned to the ancient spiritual path of shamanism. There I found powerful techniques for bringing back parts of the life-energy that might otherwise remain out of reach for years.

In *Soul Retrieval,* we will explore the shamanic belief that part of our essential life-energy can split off and become lost in "nonordinary reality." We will travel with the shamanic practitioner as, in an altered state of consciousness, he or she enters nonordinary reality in pursuit of lost soul parts.

EXAMPLES OF SOUL LOSS

Although the term *soul loss* may be unfamiliar to you, examples of it are well known under other names. A beloved spouse, child, or friend dies, and the survivor also "deadens" for a while. We feel as if the light has gone from our existence, as if we are sleepwalking. Or we return from having major surgery and do not feel as if we have come fully out of the anesthesia. A client who had been involved in a serious automobile accident reported feelings of being "spaced out."

A person involved in an abusive intimate relationship may be aware of being locked into destructive patterns but feel too weak and powerless to move away. Or in leaving the relationship, he or she might feel as though something was left behind with the partner. After a workshop, a student of mine said that since breaking up with her boyfriend she felt as though "a part of me is still with him."

The soul may leave a child who does not feel loved, or who feels abandoned, by his or her parents. In one of my clients, soul loss was caused by a parent's continual yelling, in another, by the physical pain of falling off a bicycle. A soul might leave the body to survive physical or sexual abuse. In each of these cases, the traumatized person literally escapes to survive the ordeal. Being sickly as a child or suffering serious or chronic illness can often indicate soul loss.

Literature is full of out-of-body experiences in the wake of illness or accident. Less seriously, many of us have had the experience of receiving some jolt, whereby a part of us seemed to spin out of conscious reality for a while. *Shock* is the word usually used to describe this condition. The reaction is normal and in itself no cause for alarm. But often, for reasons we don't fully understand, the part of the self that left fails to return.

What are the results? "I'm not all here," one of my clients said. "A part of me observes with my mind, but I don't connect with emotional feelings." Persons experiencing soul loss frequently say that they feel fragmented in some way or that an essential part of themselves is missing. This describes a person who is dissociated. (In clinical terms, dissociation is the separation of whole segments of the personality from the mainstream of consciousness and can result in feelings of estrangement and depersonalization.)

Another sign of soul loss is a gap in memory. I often work with men and women who have no memory of their lives from age seven through nine or twelve through fourteen. Or a person may recall that there was a trauma but can't remember the surrounding details. I once worked with a man who broke his arm and had no memory of feeling any pain at the time of the incident. Breaking an arm hurts. It hurts a lot! From a shamanic point of view, the part of my client that couldn't handle the pain simply left. I worked with a woman who knew she was an incest survivor but was unclear about the experience and could remember no details, including the act itself. She had spent years in psychotherapy trying to recapture the memories, but the part of herself that held the memories had left, so the information was not available to her.

Chronic depression is another symptom of soul loss. Often the fragmentation of a person's essential being keeps him or her from being able to create a path of joy. Life is spent exploring ways, often abusive ways, to get to feelings and experiences that create a sense of purpose, however false. Instead of being able to follow the soul's journey, such a person often feels depressed and unfulfilled.

When a divorce or death occurs, a period of grief usually ensues. After a while, life resumes some semblance of normality. If a person cannot get over the emotional trauma of separation, a red flag goes up for me: Has a piece of the self been lost?

Physical illness can also be a symptom of soul loss. Often when we give away our power we become ill. Because the universe cannot stand a void, if we are missing pieces of ourselves, an illness might fill in that place. Coma is an extreme example of soul loss.

In some way, most of us experience some degree of soul loss. Some people have been more deeply traumatized by life; they may seem quite "dispirited." Life has been kinder to others; they may not have needed to protect themselves so completely. Regardless of the degree of trauma, however, most people I know yearn for a fuller sense of vitality and connectedness to life. Soul retrieval is for everyone who wants to deepen his or her connection to self, to loved ones, to the earth.

MY OWN SOUL LOSS

Long before I trained in shamanic techniques, or worked with hundreds of clients, I had to deal with my own experience of soul loss. In the shamanic tradition of the "wounded healer," I began not by learning theory or observing others, but by coming to terms with my personal distress. To give you a deeper sense of what soul loss can feel like, I want to describe my own experience.

In childhood I was thoroughly contented. I did not know there was any other way to be. As far back as I can remember, I had a deep love of nature. I was delighted to sing and whistle to the birds and the clouds. Every day on the way home from school, I stopped at the big oak tree in front of our house and sang songs to it. I spent hours in my room, happily writing stories and drawing pictures. I was absorbed in the flow of going to school and playing with my friends outdoors. I loved my parents.

By adolescence, something had changed. Thrown into the physical and emotional turmoil of puberty, I lost the physical coordination that I had enjoyed as a child. Confused about who I was and about my place in the world, I fell from the grace that had permeated my early experience.

This kind of stress is hardly unusual in adolescence, but apparently I suffered a deeper than normal loss, and as I got older, life did not get easier. Struggling with chronic emotional depression and a sense of physical depletion, I never had any energy to spare. I no longer knew how it felt to be "in the body" in a healthy, vital way.

I used to watch people and quietly wonder to myself whether they felt as bad as I did. Did everybody feel this awkward disconnection from the body? Did everyone feel distanced from the flow of life? I knew from my childhood that there was another way of being in the world, but I had no idea how to get back to that state. I often felt that life was not worth living.

TRYING TO RECONNECT

Being the kind of person who has to do everything for myself, I never sought psychotherapeutic help. Perhaps on some unconscious level, I knew that my crisis was fundamentally spiritual. I was searching for the experience of a sacred connection with life, which I had lost.

With this connection broken, people often turn to alcohol or other mind-altering drugs. As a child of the 1960s, I thought that drugs might help fill the void. Under the influence of psychedelics, I once again caught a glimpse of the sacredness of all life and felt a deep rekindling of my love for God.

One problem with drugs was that I journeyed so far out of time and space that I could not translate my experience back into ordinary life. Drug experiences were far removed from the simple pleasures of singing to a tree on the way home from school or feeling fully alive and connected to my body. Another inescapable problem with drugs was reorienting myself back to everyday life. As the ecstatic high evaporated, I crashed into darkness. Time and time again, my attempt to escape from depression led to a reenactment of my original fall from grace.

From my subsequent experience as a counselor and workshop leader, I know that my experiences are not unusual. The story of Adam and Eve expelled from the Garden has haunted the art and literature of Western culture; it touches us deeply because it recalls the archetypal fall from grace that we each experience. Each of us, in his or her own way, becomes separated from paradise. In the shaman's language, we lose our souls.

We each have our own unique encounter with soul loss. Some falls from grace are less dramatic than mine was. I was lucky to have had an extended childhood experience of how joyful life can be. Some people are less tortured than I was by the contrast between what is *possible* and what *is*. Others, in becoming aware of their spiritual isolation, undergo what Christian mystics call "the dark night of the soul."

My own journey to recapture my soul led me on various spiritual quests. The answer that I was seeking was found in the ancient tradition of shamanism and, in particular, a contemporary revival of shamanic techniques led by the anthropologist Michael Harner, who has been my teacher and mentor. These techniques can coexist with a variety of religious beliefs. Having my own lost soul parts restored to me brought me back to a place of wholeness. I experienced the fullness of life and a joy that I had not been sure I would ever feel again.

THE PATH OF THE SHAMAN

Judging by artifacts, scientists believe that shamanic cultures extend back tens of thousands of years, long before people began to write down their history. Although these cultures differed in art, mythology, laws, economics, and social mores, they had certain universal features. In shamanic cultures, all things are thought to be permeated by Spirit. Every earthly form is animated with its own soul or life force. The well-being of any particular life-form is dependent on its spiritual harmony with other forms. Imbalances or displacement in the spiritual essence of a living being can cause debilitation and disease.

For shamans the world over, illness has always been seen as a spiritual predicament: a loss of soul or a diminishment of essential spiritual energy. If the soul totally vacates the patient, the patient will die. It follows that, if the shaman can retrieve the lost soul parts, the individual can be restored to harmony and well-being. This retrieval is done by the shaman in an altered state of consciousness. According to Mircea Eliade, an historian of religion,

> *The principal function of the shaman in Central and North Asia is magical healing. Several conceptions of the cause of illness are found in the area, but that of the "rape of the soul" is by far the most widespread. Disease is attributable to the soul's having strayed away or been stolen, and treatment is in principle reduced*

to finding it, capturing it, and obliging it to resume its place in the patient's body. Only the shaman . . . sees the spirits and knows how to exorcise them; only he recognizes that the soul has fled, and is able to overtake it in ecstasy and return it to the body.[2]

The word *shaman,* originating from the Tungus tribe of Siberia, means "one who sees in the dark." The shaman uses the ability to see "with the strong eye" or "with the heart" to travel to hidden spirit worlds to find information and to perform acts that will heal an ailing individual (or the community).

In addition to soul theft or rape of the soul, some shamanic cultures relate soul loss to interference by ghosts as well as by other human beings. In South America, according to Eliade, shamans in both the Andes and the Amazon believe that the soul can either stray away under frightening conditions or be abducted by a spirit or a ghost.[3]

MODERN CAUSES OF SOUL LOSS

As a modern practitioner of shamanism, I share many of the beliefs and perceptions of the traditional path. For me, as for the ancient ones, all creation is filled with Spirit. Human beings, animals, plants, and minerals all have their own spiritual essence with which we can communicate and interact. When any living creature is fully infused with its own spiritual force or soul, it will radiate energy and vitality. Any creature whose spirit is fully at home in its body will feel a deep resonance with that same spirit in other living things. By contrast, when any creature loses a part of its spiritual essence, a profound depletion and alienation from the rest of creation occurs.

I have met many people who appear to be suffering from loss of their spiritual essence or soul: in fact, almost everyone I have ever met suffers from some sense of incompleteness and emptiness. They sense that parts of themselves are missing and that they are cut off from a deep connection with life. For some people, this feeling of incompleteness and alienation causes great suffering. For most, the sense of not being fully alive is a continual, low-grade pain often masked with drugs, entertainment, compulsive sex, and addictions of many other kinds.

Although I share the traditional shamanic vision of soul loss, I do not usually see it as the result of theft by a magician or a wandering spirit. However, as a modern woman, I do not have to search far to find the modern equivalents of these classical concepts. Today's soul loss springs from the traumas of modern life. Incest, physical abuse, rape, loss of a loved one, accidents, wartime experiences, major illness, and surgery are assaults that can catapult the soul from the body. Faced with these kinds of stresses, the sensitive human soul may flee the body, never to return. We jokingly say of some people, "Nobody's home." This is no joke. Few of us are fully home, and some of us have been so badly traumatized that, indeed, almost no one is at home.

FROM DISSOCIATION TO SOUL LOSS

Contemporary psychology, like shamanism, recognizes that parts of the self can become separated, leaving the individual estranged from his or her essential self. Many current therapies understand that if trauma is too severe, parts of the vital, feeling self will split off to lessen the impact of the trauma. In *Healing the Shame That Binds You,* John Bradshaw explains that the incest victim "leaves the body because the pain and humiliation are unbearable." For Bradshaw, as for other purveyors of psychology, individuals dissociate as a defense mechanism when "the trauma is so great and the fear so terrifying that one needs immediate relief."[4]

Modern psychological literature is full of reports of this splitting off from the body in times of stress. Women who have been raped have reported watching their experience from a distant point on the ceiling. For months or years after the rape, they have reported feeling as if they're "not in their bodies."

Years after their return from Vietnam, many veterans began to reexperience the painful wartime events that they had "forgotten." Triggered by sounds, smells, or sights in the veteran's current life, these memories were frighteningly vivid, sometimes more vivid than the individual's current reality. Grief and rage, split off during the original trauma, often accompanied these intrusive moments.

So far, psychology and my approach to soul retrieval seem to be walking side by side. Where do they veer away from each other?

For the psychologist, the split-off parts are lost in a vast, undifferentiated region called the unconscious. This region may be teeming with dissociated memories, forbidden primal impulses, or archetypal religious imagery, depending on the psychologist's school of thought. In the case of dissociation, the job of the psychologist is to help the patient recover the lost experience. Dream work, fantasy, free association, or hypnosis might be used to help the patient gain access to these lost parts of the self.

For the psychologist, the nature and topography of the place where the split-off parts go is relatively unimportant. Conceptualized as a place beyond the light of rational consciousness, the unconscious is regarded as an undifferentiated region from which the client, with the help of the therapist, must rescue dissociated contents.

For the shaman, the question of where the split-off parts go is essential to the cure. In the shamanic worldview, vital parts of the self do not go into an undifferentiated, no-man's-land when they leave the self. Rather, the soul parts live a parallel existence in nonordinary worlds. Soul parts may be trapped in a fearful place in nonordinary reality, or they may have found more pleasant worlds where they want to stay. In any case, an important part of healing is retrieving the lost soul parts from these nonordinary worlds and returning them to the body of the patient. For the shaman, knowledge of the topography of nonordinary reality is crucial to the cure. Like explorers adventuring in difficult earthly terrains, shamans must know how to conduct themselves appropriately in nonordinary worlds if they are to perform their work successfully. The more complete one's map of the territories of nonordinary reality, the greater one's success as a shaman.

A comparison of the psychologist and the shaman at work might be helpful here. Imagine both are working with a woman suffering from multiple personality disorder, a psychological condition in which many independent personalities exist within one individual. The psychologist might say that this person has undergone very severe trauma that has necessitated splitting off or dissociating from parts of herself. He or she might suggest that these split-off parts carry memories or aspects of the personality that are not safe for the patient to experience or express.

At this point, however, the psychologist might see his or her work as helping the patient to retrieve those lost parts from her own unconscious by a slow process of uncovering and integrating. The psychologist would probably have little interest in whether those split-off parts are living in a parallel reality or, if so, in the nature of that parallel reality.

Although I feel that this kind of recovery work is extremely important, my main interest as a shamanic practitioner would be different. Where are those parts now? How can I retrieve those parts for the patient? These are the questions with which I would be most concerned. My knowledge of nonordinary reality, carefully logged in earlier journeys, would help me make the necessary journey in the most expedient, effective way.

SUPPORT FOR THE CONCEPT OF SOUL LOSS

The relevance of soul loss to our modern condition has not escaped the attention of some innovative psychologists. In her article "The Wounded Healer," for example, Jeanne Achterberg wrote,

> Soul loss is regarded as the gravest diagnosis in the shamanic nomenclature, being seen as a cause of illness and death. Yet it is not referred to at all in modern Western medical books. Nevertheless, it is becoming increasingly clear that what the shaman refers to as soul loss—that is, injury to the inviolate core that is the essence of the person's being—does manifest in despair, immunological damage, cancer, and a host of other very serious disorders. It seems to follow the demise of relationship with loved ones, career, or other significant attachments.[5]

Many Jungian therapists have found a resonance between the concept of soul loss and their work. Marie Von Franz, a prominent Jungian analyst, wrote,

> Soul loss can be observed today as a psychological phenomenon in the everyday lives of the human beings around us. Loss of soul appears in the form of a sudden onset of apathy and listlessness; the joy has gone out of life, initiative is crippled, one feels empty, everything seems pointless.[6]

A CHECKLIST OF SYMPTOMS

As you have been reading, you have perhaps been wishing for a summary of specific indicators of soul loss. The following questions are helpful in determining whether soul loss has occurred. To see whether soul loss is an issue for you and, if so, how it manifests in your life, you may want to ask yourself the following questions:

1. Do you ever have a difficult time staying "present" in your body? Do you sometimes feel as if you're outside your body observing it as you would a movie?

2. Do you ever feel numb, apathetic, or deadened?

3. Do you suffer from chronic depression?

4. Do you have problems with your immune system and have trouble resisting illness?

5. Were you chronically ill as a child?

6. Do you have gaps in your memory of your life after age five? Do you sense that you may have blacked out significant traumas in your life?

7. Do you struggle with addictions to, for example, alcohol, drugs, food, sex, or gambling?

8. Do you find yourself looking to external things to fill up an internal void or emptiness?

9. Have you had difficulty moving on with your life after a divorce or the death of a loved one?

10. Do you suffer from multiple personality syndrome?

If you answer yes to any of these questions, you may be dealing with soul loss. Important parts of your essential core self may not be available to you. If so, the vital energy and gifts of these parts are temporarily inaccessible. From my perspective, the lost parts exist in nonordinary reality, from which they can be recovered only by shamanic means.

In this chapter, we have discussed the ancient concept of soul loss and how it relates to modern-day suffering. Fortunately, shamanism provides not only a diagnosis and description of this widespread problem, but also a powerful treatment. In the next chapter, we will explore the shamanic practice of soul retrieval, which, as recent clinical experience shows, is no less applicable today than it was at the dawn of humanity.

Soul Retrieval

Souls wander the universe

Lost or stolen

Cut off from loved ones

Split off from love

Gently, carefully

We call them back to us

Searching for them in dark corners

Blowing them to life

with our breath

We welcome

them home

—Ellen Jaffe Bitz

CHAPTER 2

SOUL RETRIEVAL

*People say that what we are all seeking is the
meaning for life. I don't think that's what we're
really seeking. I think what we're seeking is
an experience of being alive.*
—*Joseph Campbell, in an interview with Bill Moyers*

Most of us are looking for a strong sense of self. We find that
the only feelings of wholeness come from within. We find
that outer security is false and that we must feel secure inside ourselves. When we are all here, or home, it's much easier to feel
peaceful and secure and in harmony with the greater whole—the
universe. We can look to nature to give us an example of this.
Here is a short exercise to help you feel what it is like to be solid
and secure.

*Close your eyes, and take four deep breaths. Take an inventory of your
body, and make a note of any place where you are experiencing pain or
tension. Send your breath to any blocked areas, and allow the tension to
release. Take your time in doing this so you can truly allow your body to
relax.*

*Imagine yourself going to a place you love in nature, where you feel very
filled up with energy. The thought of this place brings you a sense of*

*calmness and joy. Walk around, expanding your vision 360 degrees,
and take in all you see. Allow yourself to really feel being in this place.
Feel the air on your skin. Is it wet or dry, warm or cold? Feel your feet on
the ground, and wiggle your toes in the earth. Touch the earth. Listen to
all the sounds. Do you hear water running or the wind blowing? Are
there sounds of life here, or is it very still? Smell all the smells.*

*Now look around and find a tree you can sit with. Ask the tree permis-
sion to sit with it for a while, and if it says yes, sit down on the ground,
leaning your back against the tree and feeling the solid support you
have. Take a symbolic journey inside the tree, starting with the root
system. Imagine being able to suck water up through your roots, bringing nutrients to every part of the tree and through your entire body. Feel
how you start to pulsate with life and energy as each cell is being fed.
Allow that energy to move throughout your body as you experience its
moving through the trunk of the tree, into its branches, and through
your own extremities, feeding the leaves and the fruit that represent
life—feeding your life. Feel your connection with all of life. You are part
of a greater whole. None of us is here alone.*

*Really lean back into the tree and experience the love of the universe.
Know that you are right now being given guidance on how to find the
tools to bring you to a place of wholeness.*

W hen parts of a soul split off and vanish into nonordinary reality, leaving a person in a weakened, dispirited condition, it is the
job of the shaman to restore wholeness. In order to bring back
what is missing, the shaman must leave everyday consciousness
and venture into the spirit world. From the classical shamanic
viewpoint, the spirit world is a complex, multidimensional land
full of potential dangers for the uninitiated. Only a shaman is able
to navigate skillfully among the beauties and the dangers found
there. For thousands of years, the shaman's calling has been to

journey to these inner spirit worlds in order to obtain information for healing and to retrieve the lost souls of patients. Eliade has written of the spiritual vocation of the shaman:

> *Everything that concerns the soul and its adventure, here on earth*
> *and in the beyond, is the exclusive province of the shaman.*
> *Through his own pre-initiatory and initiatory experience, he knows*
> *the drama of the human soul, its instability, its precariousness; in*
> *addition, he knows the forces that threaten it and the regions to*
> *which it can be carried away. If shamanic cure involves ecstasy, it*
> *is precisely because illness is regarded as a corruption or alienation*
> *of the soul.* [1]

DRUMMING AND THE SHAMAN'S JOURNEY

When shamans "journey," they are being transported not outwardly around the face of the earth, but inwardly by the pulse of rhythmic sound. Instead of moving their bodies by ordinary physical means, they move into an altered state of consciousness in which they experience realities outside our normal perception. Michael Harner refers to this altered state as the Shamanic State of Consciousness (SSC). Typically, it is drumming that helps the shaman to enter the SSC.[2] Although some cultures use other percussion instruments, such as rattles or sticks, the shaman's drum, in Jeanne Achterberg's words, "reigns as the most important means to enter other realities, and as one of the most universal characteristics of shamanism."[3]

Why drumming has this kind of powerful effect is not clearly understood. However, scientists have discovered that listening to a monotonous beat facilitates the production of brain waves in the alpha and theta ranges, in contrast to the beta waves characteristic of ordinary, eyes-open consciousness. According to Maxwell

Cade's inventory of an electroencephalograph called the Mind Mirror, theta waves (4–7 cycles per second) are related to creativity, vivid imagery, and states of ecstasy.[4]

The link between shamanic drumming and a remarkable elevation in production of theta waves was demonstrated in a personal session with Anna Wise, who is the protégée of Maxwell Cade and the leading North American expert on the Mind Mirror. After being hooked up to the electroencephalograph, I was asked to establish baselines by sitting quietly with my eyes open, then closing my eyes and meditating, and then imagining certain colors and scenes. The brain waves associated with these activities did not differ from those of other people. However, when I began drumming and went into an altered state, as I have done thousands of times before in shamanic consultations and workshops, the amplitude of theta waves, particularly in the right hemisphere of my brain, shot to the top of the Mind Mirror's scale.

Many Native Americans refer to drumming as "the heartbeat of the earth." In this regard, it is remarkable that the electromagnetic resonance frequency of the earth, which has been measured at 7.5 cycles per second, is equivalent in brain waves to high theta/low alpha.[5] It appears that drumming allows shamans to align their brain waves with the pulse of the earth.

OTHER TOOLS OF THE TRADE

In addition to drums and rattles, shamans in many parts of the world have sacred tools to help them in retrieving souls. For example, the *manang* (a Southeast Asian shaman) has a box containing a set of magical objects, of which the most important are quartz crystals, known as "stones of light." In neoshamanism, contemporary practitioners often use crystals to light up nonordinary reality. They may also have "medicine bags," which are

This soul catcher has large toothed, wolflike heads at each end and a humanoid face in the middle. It resembles the Kwakiutl supernatural being, Sisiutl, whose usual form is a serpent with a head at each end of his body and a humanoid face in the center. This soul catcher appeared in a collection in the National Museum of Natural History of the Smithsonian. Permission to publish *Tsimshian Soul Catcher* courtesy of the Smithsonian Insitution.

pouches containing objects related to their power animal. Shamans working with a bear guardian might keep a bear claw close to them during their journeys.

Shamans in some cultures also use objects called "soul catchers." For instance, the Tsimshian shamans of British Columbia used a soul catcher carved from hollowed-out bone. Likewise, Eliade refers to a Tungus shaman of Siberia using a noose to retrieve a fugitive soul.[6]

GUARDIANS AND HELPING SPIRITS

Classically, the shaman does not make his or her inner journey alone. Power animals and other helping spirits, as well as elemental forces of nature, help the shaman carry out the work to be done. Eliade explains:

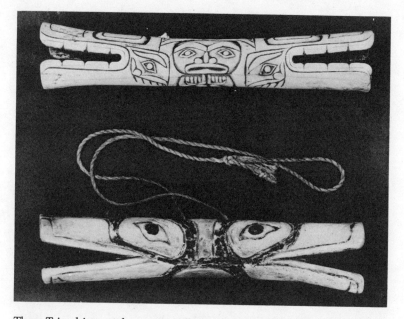

These Tsimshian catchers were collected from the Nass River in British Columbia by W. A. Newcomb in 1905. Carved from hollowed bone, these soul catchers also represent the Sisiutl, or double-breasted serpent motif, which is widespread throughout pre-Colombian cultures and the Andes. This motif is also found in the tomb art of China during the Han Dynasty, 202 B.C. to A.D. 200. Permission to publish *Tsimshian Soul Catchers* given by National Museums of Canada, Canadian Museum of Civilization, neg. # 101382.

Abandoning his body, [the shaman's] soul enters the underworld and goes in search of the patient's soul. . . . If the patient's soul has been carried off by one of the dead the shaman sends one of his helping spirits to seek it. The helping spirit catches it and brings it back. . . . If the patient's soul has been carried off by an evil spirit, the shaman is obliged to undertake the journey of recovery, which is far more difficult.[7]

Shamans believe that each human being has one or more special guardians, which protect and empower him or her.[8] (Although these guardians may be fairies or leprechauns, they usually take an animal form.) An individual's guardian, also known as a power animal, might be bear, eagle, horse, dolphin, or lion, for example. Each animal has its own area of mastery and its own unique powers that it teaches us. Eagle might teach how to view the world from a detached, aerial perspective or how to ride the subtle currents of life. Lion might teach the power of stalking prey and the fierceness of protecting cubs.

These animals appear to us as female or male and often have very distinct personalities. One of the greatest gifts for me in working with the shamanic journey has been the beautiful partnership that has evolved between my power animal and me.

The job of a power animal is to keep its charge healthy—physically, emotionally, mentally, and spiritually—by providing guidance and support. In day-to-day life anyone can call on his or her power animal when extra energy or assistance is needed, or in a dangerous place, or in a time of illness.

Like other people, a shaman calls on his or her power animal for personal assistance in ordinary reality. However, shamans also rely on them for support during spiritual journeys. Part of the power animal's job is helping the shaman navigate nonordinary reality. A power animal may provide direct information about what is wrong, about how to alleviate illness, or about steps the client needs to take in ordinary reality. If the shaman finds the soul part in a land that is difficult to enter or leave, it can be invaluable to have scouting, advice, and other assistance from the power animal. The power animal may directly assist in transporting the lost soul back to ordinary reality, for example.

A shaman may have several power animals at any given time, and a power animal may stay with a shaman for many years, perhaps for almost a lifetime. As a shaman and a power animal interact over time, the shaman learns the areas in which the power animal excels and when to call upon particular guardians. For instance, I have one guardian who is better at advising about my patients and another who is better about my own life.

In addition to guardians who are trusted spirit-friends over a long period of time, the shaman is aided by helping spirits who come for a specific purpose during a specific journey. If a shaman needs to get an aerial view of a client's situation, an eagle might swoop in and carry the shaman to the heights needed to view the situation. An elf might appear and whisper a missing piece of information in the shaman's ear. Perhaps the shaman encounters a vast sea that must be crossed to reach the client's soul. A whale or dolphin helper might appear to help.

NONORDINARY REALITY

When shamans enter nonordinary reality, the rules of the outer world are suspended. Horses fly, plants talk, fairies and leprechauns abound. Time as we know it is suspended. Shamans may, in ordinary time, spend half an hour journeying, but during that journey they may watch the sun rise and set. Outer rules of space are equally voided in these nonordinary worlds. With the aid of a spirit helper, great distances can be crossed in a moment or two of outer time.

As shamans make thousands of journeys over the years, some territories become quite familiar to them. Once a shaman has visited a place such as the Cave of the Lost Children, he or she knows the workings of that place and how to best navigate it next time. It becomes part of the shaman's map.

Shamans often have power places in nonordinary reality. Just as we have places in the outer world that make us feel peaceful, happy, and contented, so shamans have places in inner reality where they can relax and reflect. On my journeys into inner reality, for example, I often go to a dense pine forest surrounding a waterfall that pours into a great pool of water. My power animal lives there with friendly fairies, elves, and deer. I sit on rocks and gaze over the treetops at the blue sky. I lie on the soft, cool earth and safely reexperience many feelings from ordinary life. As I lie on the ground, I may feel as if my heartbeat is synchronizing with the heartbeat of the earth and feel my connection with all life.

Other journeys are like a *Star Trek* adventure as shamans encounter places and beings with whom they are less familiar. Shamans may find themselves in barren deserts that seem to extend forever. They may find unearthly cacti in this desert that speak to them about how to heal the patient. Shamans may find themselves near a cave in which a tribal African ritual is occurring and be invited to participate by a wise woman who approaches. Eliade has classified nonordinary reality into three major territories: Upper World, Middle World, and Lower World. The names come from the direction of travel the shaman experiences in getting to these worlds.[9]

There are many levels in the Upper World and Lower World. Traveling in these territories, the shamanic practitioner realizes that we live in an unlimited universe. Although descriptions of nonordinary reality are subject to mental limitations, I will share some of what I experience there to give you an idea of what these territories might be like.

The Upper World is experienced by some as ethereal. The lighting is often very bright, and the colors can go from blinding light to soft pastels, to gray, to complete darkness. In the Upper World I know that I am standing on something but am often unsure what is holding me there. I might come across a crystalline city with intricate buildings of chambers made of crystal and glass. Or there might be a lake to lie beside, or a city of clouds. Power an-

A Visit to the Lower World

imals live here, as well as teachers in human form who can offer wise guidance on human relationships.

In sharp contrast to the noncorporeal Upper World, the Lower World is reached through a tunnel leading down into the earth.[10] Although nonordinary beings and occurrences are the rule here, the landscapes are often recognizably earthy: caves, seas, dense jungle, and forests. I can stick my fingers into the earth here. The beings inhabiting the Lower World are the spirits of plants and animals, as well as human spirits who are connected with the mysteries of the earth.

The Middle World is recognizable as our own biosphere but transposed into a nonordinary key. In the Middle World the shaman can travel back and forth through human histories. Sometimes the soul of a patient has remained in a past moment of his or her life while the outer world has continued to move onward. To rescue such a soul, the shaman must travel through the Middle World to this encapsulated moment and then find a way to get the soul out of it.

METHODS FOR BRINGING BACK A SOUL

The shaman, led by an intention to retrieve the lost soul of the client, travels in nonordinary reality until he or she finds the errant soul. Once the lost soul is encountered, as I have explained, the shaman's job is to bring it back to ordinary reality.

But how? Traditional shamans used trickery, cajolery, theft, or the spirit-implements mentioned earlier to catch or snare the lost soul. Given the malevolent forces that most traditional shamans held responsible for soul loss—such as possession by the dead, rape, or theft by an ill-intentioned human—this kind of reciprocal chicanery perhaps made sense.

My own view of soul loss is influenced by contemporary psychological understanding. The soul loss with which I work is most often the result of physical and emotional trauma in which there are no clear-cut villains. The trauma that causes soul loss is often inflicted by people who are victims of their own traumas. I point this out not to excuse the perpetrator but to draw attention to the great chain of soul loss, as one generation passes its injury on to the next.

In the case of incest, for instance, the perpetrating parent is often an incest survivor. Part of the parent's soul has been lost since his or her own traumatic childhood. To know this does not make the perpetrator's actions less horrible, but it does make them more understandable. How can parents abuse their own children without having been somehow dissociated from their own natural balance? Soul loss begets soul loss.

The same is true for the perpetrators of any violent crime. These crimes can be heinous, causing great damage to the victims. After feeling empathy with the victims, one always wonders, How did the criminals become so dissociated from human feeling? What are the causes of their obvious soul loss?

Soul loss is an adaptive strategy to the original trauma. Leaving the body is at times the most intelligent way to escape the full weight of a particular horror. Whether it is a woman being raped or a man confronted with the brutalities of war, this adaptation can help the person to survive. Likewise, a small child, dependent on parents for survival, cannot physically leave an abusive situation and must find a way to minimize the pain. It always touches me to hear a person say, "I put my soul in a safe place where no one can hurt it." When a soul catapults from the body, an intrinsic intelligence is at work.

NEGOTIATING RATHER THAN TRICKING

As a practitioner, I do not feel comfortable with capturing and dragging back a soul in the way some traditional shamans are said to have done. I feel that the choice to return must come from the soul itself once it learns how the original situation has changed. I will do anything honest that I can to convince that soul to return. I explain to the lost entity that things have changed since childhood and they now have much more control over their lives. Occasionally I remind them of the good things that their early lives provided and use those pleasures as an incentive for returning. I may acknowledge their former pain and terror while I gently negotiate for their return into the present.

Sometimes the soul parts have found a pleasant spirit world that is much preferable to the one they left behind, and they don't want to return. Sometimes, the soul has fled to another world that is not particularly pleasant but in which the soul is lost or trapped. In either case, it is my job to make the soul part understand that its proper place is at home in the body of the client.

RETURNING TO ORDINARY REALITY

The traditional shaman may recount some of the events that have occurred on the journey, thus helping the client understand the nature of his or her ailment. If the shaman has received guidance on particular herbs or physical remedies that can further the healing of the client, they will be suggested.

In a similar way, I often share with the client various details I have experienced on my journey. I am cautious, however, about how much I share. If I don't know, for example, that a client is aware of incest in his or her background, I would not share any abuse information that I receive on a journey.

Often when I share an image or scene from a journey, the client feels a profound resonance. Even when certain imagery does not make logical or literal sense in terms of the client's life, I find that the information generally has soothing, healing effects that neither the client nor I fully understand on a conscious level. This is one of the mysteries of the work.

SOUL RETRIEVAL AND PSYCHOTHERAPY

As you have been reading this chapter, perhaps you have been interested but a bit unsettled by the approaches used in this kind of healing. In some ways shamanism differs drastically from the methods of psychotherapy, and in our modern age, after all, our assumptions about the healer-client relationship are profoundly influenced by psychology.

We are all familiar with the image of the client lying on the couch while the psychoanalyst sits off to the side listening. Whether in books or movies or on television, this cultural image symbolizes a specific type of human exploration in which a client actively journeys into interior worlds of dreams and memories while a therapist catalyzes, observes, guides, and supports this process.

Our prevalent model of psychological healing is based on the model of a client actively ferreting into his or her own past in order to uncover trauma that has been lodged deep in the psyche, concealed or obscured by defenses. Whether through free association in Freudian work, dreams or artwork in Jungian therapy, or hypnosis in hypnotherapy, a vehicle is introduced that allows the client to make the journey into the unconscious. In a sense, the client is the shaman traveling to retrieve his or her own lost soul. Given this current model of healing, the world of the soul retrieval may initially seem upside down or inside out.

As someone trained in psychology, I have great sympathy with its approach. Exploring within oneself and learning the richness of one's own soul can be a valuable growth experience for almost anyone. However, for the soul to be explored, it has to be in residence. How well can psychotherapy succeed when the therapist is talking to a person who isn't home?

In my view, it is frustrating to try to understand one's own negative patterns and how to change them if there is no one there to own the negative patterns. People sometimes spend years in psychotherapy before they feel safe enough to allow their vital essence to return, if it ever returns at all.

The ancient practice of soul retrieval and modern psychology potentially have much to offer each other. By restoring lost soul parts, the shaman can give the psychotherapist a whole patient with whom to do psychological work, thus making possible faster and deeper results. Conversely, the psychotherapist can help patients build self-esteem and healthy life-patterns that allow them to stay alive and present in their body once their souls have been restored to them. Adjusting to being fully in the body again, learning healthy ways of relating to the self and others, can certainly provide a good deal of work for the psychotherapist and the client.

MY DISCOVERY OF SOUL RETRIEVAL

In the next chapter, I will lead you through some soul retrievals from my practice, so that you can experience the richness and vitality of this work. As a transition, however, I would like to share with you the story of how I discovered the astonishing process of soul retrieval.

As a graduate student in counseling psychology, I took a workshop on shamanism from Michael Harner, the anthropologist who wrote *The Way of the Shaman*. Having studied his subject the world over, Harner found certain elements common to most shamanic cultures. These elements, which he labeled "core shamanism," included induction into the Shamanic State of Consciousness (SSC) through drumming; entry into nonordinary reality through an opening in the earth; work with power animals and spirit helpers; exploration of nonordinary worlds; and practices for bringing back healing information for oneself and one's community.

From the beginning, I was profoundly moved by Harner's work. On my first journey under his direction, I met my power animal, who, to my astonishment, answered many questions about my life for me. This first journey convinced me of the power and truth of shamanism.

After the initial workshop, I decided to practice journeying with a group of friends. We met weekly, sitting in a circle, taking turns drumming for one another, and sharing our experiences. Once I had gained confidence with this method, I began to teach it to certain clients in my counseling practice. It was, I discovered, an effective way for people to find information for themselves, to become their own authorities. It was also a potent way to reconnect with nature and with the energizing forces of life.

After a series of trainings, I became a member of the International Faculty of Michael Harner's Foundation for Shamanic Studies. I eventually taught courses across the United States, in Australia and New Zealand, and in Austria, Denmark, and Switzerland.

During my first years of shamanic practice, I taught individuals how to journey and how to work with their power animals. Later I began to teach other shamanic practices. Although I certainly knew about soul retrieval from Michael Harner's teaching and the literature, it was not yet part of my experience or teaching. In the late 1980s, however, I had an experience that introduced me to soul retrieval in a sudden and dramatic way.

A PAIR OF SMALL ARMS

In one of my workshops, a woman named Carol had, under my direction, just taken a shamanic journey to the Upper World, one of the realms that shamans often visit. Carol met a teacher in the Upper World who told her that she needed to do serious work on a trauma that she had suffered as a child. On the return from her journey, Carol told me that when she was three, she had been raped by her father. I agreed to meet with Carol the following morning to help her face this pain and, if possible, release it.

When we met, I first took a journey to confer with my power animal, who would tell me how I could help. At that time, I had already been working with this spirit for eight years and had telepathically received many wise, deeply helpful communications from him. In short, I had great confidence in the information he provided. In the session with Carol, an assistant provided the drumming, which quickly helped me into an altered state of consciousness. As the drumming began, I entered the earth through a hollow tree trunk that led into a dark tunnel deep into the Lower World. While I traveled along toward the light, I sent a strong telepathic message to my power animal to be waiting for me. I entered the Lower World in a pine forest with a river rushing by, a place that I had visited many times before and that always fills me with great peace. As I had hoped, my power animal was waiting. We sat down by the river while I told him about Carol's predicament.

In response, he took me back into Carol's life. Suddenly I found myself watching what had happened to her when she was three years old. As I watched, I saw something for which I was totally unprepared. As the rape was taking place, I saw Carol's soul, her essence, separate from her body and leave. As I watched her departing soul, I saw that it had gone into a place known in shamanism as the void—a place of pitch darkness, silence, lifelessness.

It became clear to me that Carol's soul had been in the void ever since the childhood rape. Continuing my journey, I began tracking her directly into the void, holding the intention clear that I would find her. I could not see in the blackness and so called out her name. The voice of a small child answered, "I am here."

"I can't see you," I yelled back. "Can you see me?"

"Yes," she called.

I asked her if she wanted to come back with me. "Yes," she answered, and at this point I felt a small pair of arms encircling my neck. It was time to go home. When we returned to ordinary reali-

Returning with Carol from the Void

ty, I blew the three-year-old soul into Carol's heart and the top of her head, as shamans have traditionally done. "Welcome home," I said to the part that had been lost in the void.

When I talked to Carol about my experiences, she could remember the void and could remember going there when she was three years old. She had never been able to describe this experience to anyone. She was touched that I cared enough about her to go into this dark, empty place in search for her.[11]

A few weeks after our session, Carol called me. She reported that she felt as if she were present in her body for the first time in her adult life. Whereas she always had felt disconnected from herself before, she now experienced life directly and intensely. Colors appeared more vibrant. Plants seemed as alive as animals. No longer did she experience life as a movie she was merely observing.

At that time, I had never worked with survivors of incest. I did not know that Carol's report of feeling disconnected from her body was consistent with that of other people who had suffered sexual abuse. Since that time, I have found that various kinds of trauma—accidents, illness, surgical operations, loss of loved ones, war, and abuse of any kind—may leave people feeling separated from their bodies. I have found that the souls of many children and adults are lost in the void or in other spirit worlds, and that soul retrievals can help these souls return home to the body.

Several months after I began using this method, I met Christina Crawford, author of *Mommie Dearest* and founder of the Survivors Network. She attended a workshop where I demonstrated soul retrieval. Through her travels and her work with her organization, Christina was constantly hearing about the effects of abuse. When we worked together with the soul retrieval technique, she was so impressed that she asked for further instruction and made the serious commitment necessary when learning such a powerful technique. Soon she began to integrate soul retrieval into her work with survivors.

My work, first with Carol and then later with Christina, led me to formulate certain questions. As I moved around the country teaching weekly workshops in shamanism, I wondered how many of us are separated from our souls due to trauma. I wondered to what extent the immoderate use of food and alcohol or other drugs is a misguided attempt to fill the hole created by this loss. Gradually, I began to see the connection between the psychological pain prevalent in our society and the ancient diagnosis of soul loss. These questions led me to explore the techniques of soul retrieval.

To observe how these techniques work in the modern world, you will be able, in the next chapter, to watch over my shoulder as I travel in nonordinary reality to retrieve lost soul parts for several of my clients.

I See the Children Hiding

I see the face of every broken child;
staring eyes that darkness only lights;
where do they go to play
& where lie down to nap?

I see their faces in the night
each chipped and splintered spirit
forever scarred with having run to hide.
They wait to have never been hurt.

In their eyes the tears have dried,
& puffy cheeks gone pale—
where do their spirits walk tonight?
Where is the pathway home?

I cannot drum, but drum for these,
& drumming so, for me.

—Stephen Van Buren

CHAPTER 3

TRACKING LOST SOULS

*Mother, one of your children wants to
come home. Help me bring her back
to you so that she can take her
rightful place on earth.*
—*Prayer used in soul retrievals*

As you prepare to journey with me, I invite you to light a candle. On occasions as diverse as birthday parties and church services, we use candles to lead us into a special state of being. A candle may remind us, for instance, that solid matter (the wax) is related to Spirit (the light). When I am about to enter nonordinary reality, I sometimes light a candle as a way to call upon helping spirits. Likewise, you might join me in this Spirit now by lighting a household candle, sitting with it for a moment, and leaving it lighted as you read. What could be simpler?

Light the candle. Notice, as you light it, whether you feel any subtle changes in your body. Perhaps you will gradually feel somehow lighter. Emotionally, you may feel a little safer and more peaceful. If these effects do not stand out at first, just let the candle burn, and perhaps you will feel a difference as you read.

Spirit comes into our space in response to a call. As you light your candle, know that Spirit will guide and support you as you follow me in my travels.

Your intellect can learn much about shamanism, but your heart can touch it even more deeply. Perhaps you are ready to open to shamanism—not as a belief or faith, but as an adventure that may yield results that you can verify. Your candle simply reminds you of your openness to that adventure.

*I*magine now that we are in a somewhat darkened room together. You are sitting on a beloved chair or cushion watching as I, in the middle of the room, prepare to do a soul retrieval. You see me pull out a weathered gray Zapotec blanket from Mexico decorated with a burgundy pattern.

This blanket and I are old friends. Since receiving it as a gift, I have used it in hundreds of healing sessions. Once I sat on it four days and three nights, fasting and praying for a vision. This blanket is a healing tool that helps me make the transition to nonordinary reality. When I lie on it, I feel embraced by Spirit and filled with healing power.

After I spread the blanket, you watch me place my rattle, a Native American drum, and a crystal nearby. At the beginning of each session I will rattle as I pray to the Great Mother (the feminine aspect of Spirit) to help me bring the soul of my client home. The drumming will be done by an assistant. (When there is no one to assist I use a tape of shamanic drumming. However, even then, I keep my own drum nearby.) Like the blanket, my drum has been part of many journeys. Its very presence begins to draw me into other worlds.

My crystal lies waiting also. When I begin to journey, I will keep it in my pocket to remind me that I have the ability to see what is hidden beyond ordinary awareness. It is my equivalent to the soul catchers used by traditional shamans.

As you relax in your chair and watch proceedings that may seem somewhat foreign to you, I encourage you to take a few deep breaths. The people whom you will observe are perhaps not very different, in some ways, from you. What they share is a desire for deep healing and for a greater sense of aliveness. These individuals may or may not be familiar with shamanic practices.

Settle back now in your privileged role as a safe observer. Watch with interest and curiosity as each client comes to this room for a session. In turn, Susan, Ellen, Edward, and Marsha will lie on the blanket beside me, each with shoulders, hip, and ankles touching mine. Watch me as the drumming begins, as I cover my eyes with my forearm and begin to sink into an altered state of consciousness.

For these moments, you are now given the precious gift of inner sight. You are able to watch not only the outer forms of me and my clients as we lie on the floor but also the contents of my visions as I travel into nonordinary worlds. Where I go, you will also be able to go.

There is a single exception. During each journey I will speak with my guardian animal. In the shamanic world, the identity of one's guardian often remains a treasured secret. To share it with others, except under special circumstances, would be to diffuse its power. For this reason, I will not explicitly describe my guardian to you. To make these journeys richer for yourself, you may want to visualize an animal that you love and respect and let it carry out the same actions that my guardian does.

And now the first client knocks on the door. She is Susan.

THE LITTLE GIRL WHO DIDN'T WANT TO COME HOME

Susan is a drug and alcohol abuse counselor. Like many counselors, she is in therapy herself, both to facilitate her own healing and to hone her professional sensitivity. For some time, she has felt that her own therapy was stagnant. She and her therapist have been working with the metaphor of contacting Susan's inner child. But where is this child? Try as she might, Susan has not been able to find a child in herself. Both she and her therapist are frustrated and have agreed that Susan should try another way to reconnect with her inner child. She is here today to see if I can help her in this quest.

Before I begin to shift my consciousness by drumming, I ask Susan to show me the jewelry she is wearing. When hunting for elusive soul parts, I often find that it helps to watch for jewelry. Think about the problem. In nonordinary reality, the soul parts might not look very much like the client who comes to me for help, particularly if the soul part left in childhood. But no matter what age the soul is in nonordinary reality, her earlier self will wear the same jewelry as the client does in the present. If I can see the same ring or bracelet, I can identify the wandering soul despite any difference in years.

> Today Susan is wearing a very delicate silver ring on her right hand. After singing my power song, I lie down next to her holding in my mind's eye the intention of my journey. As the drumming begins, I begin to see myself floating up through many cloud layers until, after a few moments, I am catapulted into outer space, where I tumble about in slow motion, feeling lost in a peaceful limbo of gentle, rocking sensations. Surrounded by darkness and soft sounds, I am easily lulled into an unconscious state. Suddenly I remember my mission and break out of this state by calling to Susan.

> I look around, and as my eyes focus, I see that the darkness is filled with many planets and shining stars. Expanding my vision, I see a child's head peek out from what looks like a mass of rock floating in space. Drifting up to her as if in zero gravity, I relax and approach in a nonthreatening way. "Are you Susan?" I ask. As the child nods, I glimpse the silver ring on the right hand. She looks about seven years old.

> "Susan," I say. "I am a friend who wants to bring you home."

"No," she replies, "I don't want to go back there." She looks as though she might throw a full-blown temper tantrum.

At this point, my power animal appears beside me and shows me a scene of Susan's life in ordinary reality at the age of seven. I see these images as if I were watching an inner movie. Susan is sitting in her living room playing with dolls. Her father walks in looking bleary-eyed after a long workday. Is he just tired, or has he been drinking? I can't tell. Unfortunately, he trips over one of Susan's many toys.

"How many times do I have to tell you not to leave your toys all over the living room?" he yells. As her father came in, Susan had stood up with her hands behind her back to greet him. Now, in frustration, he slaps her. My power animal looks at me and communicates to me telepathically, "This is not the first time, nor will it be the last."

Now I turn from this scene revealed to me by my guardian and look back at little Susan hiding behind the rock. Clearly she is afraid to return with me to ordinary reality. However, my guardian has a gift for speaking gently and reassuringly to frightened little ones. "Susan," he says, "remember how much you loved to walk in the woods, singing to the trees? Remember how much you loved to jump rope and play ball?"

Hearing these words, Susan looks less frightened and gets a far-away look in her eyes. I join in and say, "You are much older now, and you don't live with your father anymore. You don't have to worry about his hitting you again. It's safe now, Susan. Will you come home with me?"

At last she agrees to return.

After we go back to ordinary reality, I sit up and blow that soul part into Susan through her chest and through the top of her head, in the traditional way. She sits up and I share with her my experiences on this journey. Since Susan seems stable emotionally and has been previously aware of abuse, I feel easy about sharing the contents of my journey with her.

(Some months from now, Susan will tell me that her session opened up a "gentle remembering" of her lost childhood, that she loves having her little girl back, and that she is no longer depressed. Most important, having the child back helps her move forward in her therapy.)[1]

JOURNEY TO THE CAVE OF THE LOST CHILDREN

As Ellen enters the room where you and I are sitting, she looks depressed and dispirited. Her report on her life confirms this: although her job as an office worker is stable, she has been involved in a series of painful, unhealthy relationships with men. Almost always angry at someone about something, she desperately wants to experience the happiness that has eluded her.

I ask Ellen whether she really wants change and whether she feels safe with me. When she answers both questions with a firm yes, I know that we are ready to begin.

After saying my prayer and lying down beside Ellen on the rug, I enter a tree trunk that leads into a cool, dark tunnel. My hair brushes against the roof of the tunnel, and I feel cool, brown dirt gently dusting my cheek. Down through the tunnel I move, silently asking my power animal to wait for me at the end. At the same time, I focus my intention to find a lost part of Ellen that would be helpful to her at this time.

As I exit from the tunnel into the light, my power animal grabs my hand so quickly that I have no time to glance around or communicate with him verbally. He begins to lead me deeper and deeper into the earth, through the realms known as the Lower

Soul Retrieval

The Cave of the Lost Children

World. I initially pay close attention to the levels we pass through but soon lose count as we travel through seemingly endless layers. As we travel, my throat constricts, and my skin feels clammy; I have a premonition of where we are going.

Finally we arrive on a level that is barren and empty. A clear blue sky eerily lights a landscape of light brown dirt that stretches toward a distant mountain. There is not a speck of green or of anything living.

My power animal and I walk together on the soft earth, feeling the absolute emptiness of the place. Slowly we approach the mouth of a cave located in a mountain, with fallen rock all around. As we enter the pitch blackness of the cave, my heart is beating fast. I know that we are in the Cave of the Lost Children, one of the most heart-wrenching places in all of the inner worlds. As my eyes adjust to the darkness, I see the outlines of hundreds of children of all races huddling together in the cave. Hundreds of huge, sad eyes—black, brown, and blue—stare at me. My heart contracts with pain as I see them in their timeless reality—lost, unwanted, and frightened. Always waiting.

I pull myself away from the pain of my response and refocus my intention to find Ellen. Soon I feel a pull on my solar plexus as if there were a rope extending from there being pulled upon. A child with strong, steel blue eyes moves toward me. She is about five years old. The darkness prevents me from seeing clearly what she is wearing.

"Are you Ellen?"

She nods her head affirmatively with no expression on her face. When I ask her whether she wants to come back with me, she grabs me so hard that her rough nails dig into my arm. I take one of her hands in mine, and my power animal holds the other, as we begin to leave the cave in single file. I'm aware of the mournful, staring eyes of the other abandoned children as we leave.

Once we are outside the cave, I lean down and wipe Ellen's dirty, tearful face with a tissue. She tells us that her parents are so concerned about their own problems that each one has forgotten her. She explains that her mother has been drinking constantly since her father left, and that there's no one to watch over her. She begins to cry, "I've been so scared."

I feel a little paralyzed by her pain, but my power animal, who is always full of surprises, steps in with just the right approach. He picks up Ellen and makes funny faces at her until she cracks a smile. Her smile eases the sadness that I have felt ever since leaving the cave.

I ask Ellen if she is ready to return to the adult Ellen who is waiting for her in ordinary reality. She says that she is almost ready but wants to ask me a question first. "Do you know why Ellen is always so angry?" I answer that I don't know. She says, "Ellen

thinks that she has to be big and angry to protect me. I don't need
protection. I just want someone to love me."

I take the child in my arms and lay her head on my shoulder.
I gently carry her into ordinary reality.

I blow the five-year-old child into the adult Ellen, then rattle around Ellen four times to seal that soul part into her body. As Ellen opens her eyes, I say to her returned soul, "Welcome home." Ellen immediately responds that she feels a welcome warmth in her solar plexus. As I share my visions with Ellen, she confirms two facts that my ordinary self had not known: her parents split up when she was five, and her mother was an alcoholic. She knows that she lost the ability to trust at that age and that this has affected her ability to experience intimacy with anyone. When I report that her little girl has said that the adult Ellen's anger is intended as a protection for the little girl, Ellen understands. As we are talking, Ellen reports that the warmth is spreading throughout her body. Her fingers and toes have begun to tingle.

(Several months from now, I will speak with Ellen again. Things are not perfect in her life, but she has made significant changes. She feels softer and more playful and generally trusts herself more. Although I am still haunted by the eyes of the abandoned children, she remembers the journey home as a great relief.)

THE BOY WITH THE PERFECT HOME

A soul doesn't always travel into the Lower World (as Ellen did) or to the Upper World (Susan). Often a soul is lost on our own level of reality, encapsulated in a past (or even future) moment. Such is the case of Edward, who is a carpenter.

He appears unsettled and disturbed as he enters the room to join us. One of his pressing difficulties is never feeling comfortable at any location where he lives. He has moved many times trying to find a place where he can feel at home, but he always feels unsettled, wondering where to go next.

I begin the journey for him with the usual prayer and rattling. I set my intention to travel wherever I need to go to retrieve the soul part that will most serve Edward's life.

As I follow the sounds of the drumbeat, I find myself outside a house near a beach. The sun is shining, the moist air filled with salt smell.

The house reminds me of a Norman Rockwell painting. Soft curtains are drawn back at the window, revealing a spotless living room. As I peek through, I see a cream-colored rug and lots of comfortable furniture. A gallery of family photographs lines the walls. Turning my attention to the rest of the neighborhood, I see one-story California-style houses. The block is very quiet now, but I imagine kids riding their bikes after school and dads washing their cars there on the weekends.

Four times I repeat my intention to find Edward's missing soul parts. My intention draws me into the house. I pass through a cool, narrow hallway into a cheerful yellow kitchen. As I walk to the back door, I can see Edward in the backyard pitching his tent. He looks like a supremely contented nine-year-old. Approaching him, I explain that I was sent to bring him home. He responds without hesitation, "But I am at home."

I explain to Edward that time has moved on and that he is no longer nine. He is a grown man of forty-three. Little Edward listens to me unhappily without the slightest interest in leaving. "But I love this place," he says tearfully, "please don't make me leave." I ask Edward where his parents are, and he answers defiantly that they have moved, "But they can't make me move from here."

Edward's current dilemma begins to become clear to me. His parents left this much-loved home when he was nine years old, and part of him stayed behind. He has never been able to feel at home anywhere because a part of him has never left his past. Unlike Ellen when I found her trapped in a sad, lonely place, little Edward is in a world that he truly loves. However, as I patiently explain, his true place is with the adult Edward, and until they are reunited, neither can be truly happy.

Little Edward looks away from me as he considers my words. The child finally asks, "Edward really wants me back, does he?" I assure him that this is true. He asks me how to get back and shyly places his hand in mine. Together we wave good-bye to his house as we return to ordinary reality.

After welcoming the soul home, I share my journey with my client. Moved by the images, he tells me that his father was transferred back east from Los Angeles when he was nine. Edward hated leaving the only home he had ever known. He could never understand his irrational pull toward Los Angeles, because he has no current intention of living there. He was sure a part of his little-boy soul had stayed with the home he had loved.

THE WOMAN WHO LOVED TO SLEEP

Watch now as Marsha enters the room. She is depleted and depressed. It is difficult to imagine where she gets the energy to help people in her work as a psychotherapist. In fact, she reports that she is not enjoying her work or her personal life. Her best times now are when she is asleep; she feels contented then. The rest of the time she feels drained and longs to return to bed.

We go through the preparatory rituals, and I firmly set my intention to bring back the lost soul parts.

*As I begin to travel, I find myself pulled up through a cloud
membrane into the Upper World. As I look around, I see
Marsha's soul looking much as she does today, climbing up a
silver rope. She is desperately trying to reach a baby that is
within her sight but out of reach. "Marsha," I ask, "where are
you going?"*

"I have to get my baby."

I have a strong intuition. "Is that baby you?"

*Marsha responds that it is. "Every night I go a little farther trying
to reach the baby. I want my baby back."*

*Marsha's predicament touches my heart. She is like Sisyphus,
who rolls a stone toward a hilltop he can never reach. Marsha
appears condemned to make an eternal climb without ever being
able to reach her baby.*

*How to help? In nonordinary reality I am quickly able to climb
the silver rope to the level that Marsha is unable to reach. There
is the baby lying on a cloud. I pick her up, and pressing her to
my chest, start down the rope with her. When I reach Marsha,
I gently place the baby in her arms.*

*"Marsha, put your hands around my waist," I instruct her. The
three of us slide down through the layers of Upper World clouds
back to ordinary reality. Holding both the adult and the baby
parts in my arms, I blow them into Marsha's chest and the
crown of her head. "Welcome home," I whisper.*

When I share the images of my journey with Marsha, she
feels moved by them, although she has little idea of why or when
her baby-self left. (When I follow up with Marsha several months
later, I will learn that she has felt an amazing resurgence of energy.
She is excited by her work and is no longer engaged in a love affair
with sleep.)[2]

Marsha's experience demonstrates that insight or understanding is not essential to this type of healing. Although she was trained in insight therapy herself, her relief had little to do with intellectual understanding of how or why the splits in her soul occurred. The crucial element seems to have been her reunion with lost parts of her self.

SOME AFTERTHOUGHTS ON MY JOURNEYS

As you have traveled with me, you have probably been making some mental notes about the nature of these inner journeys. One of the things you may have noticed most strongly is the unpredictability of this work. Although the outer rituals of preparation and return provide a predictable frame for the journey, the images of the journey are rich and varied. The pictures that will fill the frame are always a surprise.

I never know exactly where I am going to go or what is going to happen. I don't know whether I will be in the Lower, Middle, or Upper World or whether the lost soul parts will be adults, children, or (as in the case of Marsha) both. I don't know whether the soul parts will be trapped in unhappy realities or will have found more congenial places that they will be reluctant to leave. I certainly can't predict what my own responses will be. I may experience deep fright or intense joy. Places such as the Cave of the Lost Children may haunt me for years.

When I enter into nonordinary reality, I surrender my ideas of what is possible. I may receive amazingly accurate pictures of a client's early life experience, of things I have no way of knowing in ordinary reality. My job is to let go of my limiting ideas of what is possible and open fully to the places to which I am led.

How do I maintain this kind of openness? In part, I am supported and guided by the healing purpose of the journey. My intention is like an arrow flying through the pitfalls and distractions of nonordinary reality. History has taught me that a strong inner intention will lead me directly to the experience that needs to happen. If I get distracted by the soul's state (as I did when I was journeying for Susan) or by fears (as I did with Ellen), I can reset my healing intention and again begin to walk a straight path.

The other major supports are my power animals and spirit helpers—indispensable partners who guide, support, and instruct me as I enter unfamiliar territories. As you may remember, my power animal pulled me out of several impasses in the journeys that I shared with you. Simple things like picking up the frightened Ellen and making her laugh can turn a whole situation around.

As with any partnership, trust grows with repeated experiences of support and caring. I have received so much consistent wisdom and support from my guardians that I now wholly trust them. When I journey into the unknown worlds, I know that I will receive the help that is appropriate.

In my shamanic practice, the combination of consistent, stable outer rituals and rich, varied inner experience has been balancing and nourishing to me. I cannot imagine living without access to these inner worlds. I cannot imagine living without helping others to become whole through this work.

PART II

THE SEARCH

CHAPTER 4

A QUESTION OF TECHNIQUE

*In describing soul retrieval of the Ostyak Vasyugan,
Central Asia: The shaman is in no way "possessed"
by his helping spirits. As Karjalainen observes, they
whisper into his ear in just the same way in
which "birds" inspire the epic bards.*
—Mircea Eliade, Shamanism:
Archaic Techniques of Ecstasy

If you understand only the words *intention* and *trust*, you understand the key to shamanic healing. When one does a soul retrieval, it is essential to have a crystal-clear intention: What is the mission you are trying to accomplish? Likewise, it is critical to trust that you will get the spiritual assistance you need.

In shamanism (as well as with other forms of healing) it is not the shaman who does the work. Shamans are just the instruments through which the power of the universe works. Therefore, asking the spirits for help and trusting that they will be there is the basis of the shaman's responsibilities. Remember, an instrument cannot play itself.

In shamanism the power of the shamanic healing comes from the shaman's willingness to intervene in the spiritual realms on behalf of the client. The spirits take pity on the client because someone else was willing to make an effort for this person.

The hardest part for many of us doing shamanic work is the issue of trust. Our culture does not support shamanism and working with the spirits. How, then, does one just jump into the work and declare total belief in these unseen forces?

This dilemma is not unfamiliar to me. I grew up in Brooklyn in a middle-class family with strong middle-class beliefs. Sometimes in the middle of a shamanic healing, my mind will intrude and ask, "Sandy, what are you doing? Have you totally lost your mind?" I quiet my mind by repeating to myself, "This really works." Doing this allows me to reenter a deeper state of consciousness where my connection with Spirit is strong. Trust comes through experience. In over eleven years of doing shamanic journeying, I have never been let down by the spirits.

Learning to do shamanic healing takes time, lots of practice, and experience. In this chapter I will share the details of my work to demystify it for you as you read on. I do not intend to teach you how to do soul retrieval in this chapter—that, I believe, is unethical. And I feel it is just as unethical for one to try a soul retrieval after just reading this book.

If we truly want to honor the spirits and use the ancient ways in a powerful way, we must maintain integrity in the work at all times. Please do not dishonor yourselves, the people who are important to you, or the spirits by trying soul retrieval without the appropriate training.

MEETING THE CLIENT

My interview with my clients differs from a first session one might encounter in traditional psychotherapy. To do a successful soul retrieval I do not need to know a person's history. When I first started doing soul retrievals, I wasn't sure how the method worked, so for the first hundred people I worked with, I tried an experiment. I asked my clients not to tell me anything about themselves or their issues. I just explained soul retrieval and asked them to trust that they would get back the parts of themselves that they needed.

As I suspected and hoped would happen, the synchronicities were absolutely amazing. Time after time what I found out on my shamanic journeys coincided exactly with memories from a person's life. When I worked with Steven, I saw that at the age of twenty-eight he suffered a broken heart. That, I discovered, was the age at which his wife left him. In my journey for Catherine I saw her at the age of four, wearing certain clothes and desperately holding onto a Raggedy Ann doll. A few days later Catherine returned to me with the exact photograph of herself and the doll I had described. With Valerie I witnessed violence shown toward her five-year-old self by a man who appeared as a shadow with a hat. Valerie later reported to me that her grandfather had abused her. She always remembered his huge shadow on her wall at night and how she always saw his hat.

With most of the soul retrievals there was total synchronicity with the age of the trauma and with what the client remembered. Of course, there were clients who could not relate to the information. Some of the events I saw occurred before conscious memory; some clients were not yet ready emotionally to remember the events.

After about a year of working "blind," I developed greater confidence in the soul retrieval method. I became more flexible about people's sharing their histories with me. I still feel, however, that too much information actually interferes with my work, so I ask people just to summarize their main issues.

It is very important for my clients to trust me and feel safe with me. Historically, in tribal societies, there was no question about trusting the shaman. The shamans were highly respected healers in the community. Today most people who come to work with me are meeting me for the first time. I'm getting ready to actually "blow" their vital soul into their bodies. This is an incredibly intimate experience, and I want to know before I begin my journeys that my clients feel safe with me. In the United States statistics reveal that one of every three women and one of every five men have been abused.[1] I want to be certain my clients and I are working in partnership for their healing and that I am not another person doing something *to* them.

The way I establish safety is by allowing plenty of time in the session for us to talk together. This gives my clients an opportunity to get to know me as a person and decide whether they want to work with me. I also explain shamanism, the shamanic journey, power animals, and illness from a shamanic perspective so they can become more familiar with the system. Shamanism makes sense to people, so I have never found a client to be confused about how it all works.

In the session, my explanation of soul loss is relatively easy; most of my clients already feel that a piece of them is missing. They are relieved to discover that what they have been feeling most of their lives actually has a name.

Explaining the effects of soul retrieval is the hard part. I am noncommittal about the effects, because, as we shall see in chapter 8, there is such a wide range of experiences, with no way to predict what an individual client's response will be. We all have our own ways of dealing with our experiences, and I trust implicitly the way each person's being processes the information and knows the right timing for assimilating, integrating, and dealing with the memories that might surface.

Because I don't know how a person will feel after a soul retrieval, I suggest that clients schedule a time with me when they have the rest of the day free, just in case they need time alone

Soul Retrieval

afterward. I also request that people abstain from alcohol for twenty-four hours before and after the soul retrieval; I find that alcohol seems to distort the feelings that come up.

One of the most important questions I ask clients is whether they are willing to have change occur in their lives; people's lives do change after soul retrieval. What do I mean by change? I think that many people equate change with winning the sweepstakes or a similar event. Reeducation about change is often necessary. Once a person's soul is returned, there is often a need to alter any life-patterns involving relationships, family, diet, or work that are abusive or unhealthy. Most people do make the changes that will put their lives back into harmony again. (Later, in chapter 8, I will discuss this in greater detail.) But I advise clients that their lives probably will be different. If they don't want any change, then soul retrieval is not the right process for them at this time. The typical response is, "Yes, I'm ready for something to change. That's why I'm here!"

I explain to clients that I will be touching them and blowing their souls into their bodies, and I ask their permission to do this. Because many of my clients may be struggling with issues of abuse, I don't want them to perceive me as another perpetrator.

Finally, I ask about the client's support system. Who cares that the person is back home again? Who will be there if painful memories come up in the weeks to come? Who will be there to share in the celebration and joy in being home again? One way to set up an automatic support system is to have clients bring a friend or significant person to participate in the ceremony. The friend can help in the drumming, be fair witness to the process, and be there to welcome the person home.

Now that the preliminary steps are taken care of, the actual work of soul retrieval is ready to begin.

SETTING THE SPACE

Soul retrieval is a ceremony, and for this I want my space to be a certain way. The process of creating this space varies among persons doing the work. The first thing I do is light a candle in a darkened room; this act is how I request the presence of Spirit in the room.

Next I get ready anything I need to do the soul retrieval. I place my blanket on the floor for my client and me to lie on together. On the blanket I place my rattle, which will be used to call my helping spirits to me. I get out my little crystal soul catcher in case I need it. I have found that sometimes in my journey I have trouble holding onto all the soul parts. A crystal can actually act as a comfortable "waiting room" for the soul parts as I continue my journey. My crystal soul catcher is also helpful if the soul has shattered; the soul catcher acts as a vacuum cleaner to sweep up the splintered parts.

Calling My Helping Spirits

In chapter 2, I mentioned that the *manang* shamans of Southeast Asia used crystals as soul catchers; there are also illustrations of soul catchers used by the Northwest Coast people made of hollowed-out bones. Tools can sometimes be helpful, but I caution people about becoming dependent on the tools. Sometimes we forget where the true source of the power lies, and we bestow this power on our tools. In spiritual healing work, tools may be helpful but are not essential.

Next, I ask my client to lie down on the blanket. I explain that when I am ready to begin my work, I will lie next to him or her, touching shoulder, hip, and ankle.

Before I begin my journey I kneel next to my client. I whistle to call the helping spirits to me so we are all working in partnership. Then I begin to rattle and sing my power song, a song that came to me years ago. This song changes my consciousness, which is essential to move my ego and my ordinary consciousness out of the way so the work can happen. When I feel altered, I lie down next to my client.

THE JOURNEY

As I lie down next to my client, the drumming begins. Either I have someone drumming for me, or if that is not possible, I listen to a shamanic drumming tape. My client has been instructed to lie quietly, staying as "present" as possible and being receptive to the returning soul parts. The client remains passive in this stage of the process. My responsibility is tracking the soul parts and returning them to the client. The client's work starts once he or she walks out my door and begins to integrate the soul parts back into everyday life—a big job!

When the drumming begins, I repeat my intention to myself four times. For example, "I am looking for any lost parts of Jane that would be helpful to have back at this present time." If I know that there is a special issue Jane is struggling with—such as abuse, addiction, grief, or trust—I keep that information close to me so the spirits will show me the parts needed that relate to the particular problem. The drum is my path out of my body as well as my path back, but it is my intention that draws me in the shamanic journey and helps me track the client. I actually feel a physical pull in my solar plexus to go a certain direction into the Lower World, the Middle World, or the Upper World.

> When a human being has "lost his soul," the shaman works himself into ecstasy by means of a special technique; while he remains in that state, his soul travels to the world of spirits. Shamans contend to be able, for instance, to track down the lost soul in the underworld in the same way as a hunter tracks down game in the physical world. . . . Once they have recaptured the lost soul, they bring it back and restore it to the deprived body, thus achieving the cure.[2]

When I speak of going on a shamanic journey, what is it in me that journeys? In changing my awareness and shifting consciousness, my own soul leaves my body in order to enter nonordinary reality; it is the soul that does the traveling in the shamanic journey. According to the anthropologist Åke Hultkrantz, "In all of North America except the Southwest the belief recurs in one

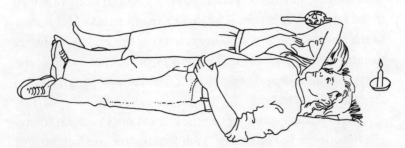

The Journey

form or another that man is equipped with two kinds of soul, one or more bodily souls that grant life, movement, and consciousness to the body, and one dream or free soul identical to man himself as he is manifested outside of his body in various psychic twilight zones."[3] I believe it is the free soul that journeys and that through soul retrievals we bring back parts of the physical soul that have been lost.

One important aspect of journeying is that a shaman journeys at will. A shaman goes into nonordinary reality at will and comes back to ordinary reality at will. A shaman doesn't get stuck but jumps back and forth between realities with discipline that is learned, constantly practiced, and constantly tested.

Tracking a person's soul is not as hard as it sounds. Again this is where intention and trust is crucial, because the shaman has no idea if the soul is lost in the Upper, Middle, or Lower World.

One has lots of help in the journey. Sometimes I actually feel as if I have too much help. My power animal is giving me directions. I often meet the spirit of my client in nonordinary reality. Although I ask my clients to stay present in their bodies during a soul retrieval, they very rarely do and instead come along to help. Then, as we shall see in subsequent case studies, soul parts that I have already found give me information. When I worked with Charles, his five-year-old part told me I needed to find his nine-year-old part in the Upper World.

In doing a soul retrieval I receive information in a variety of ways, never knowing beforehand how the information will come. Sometimes I am shown the scene and details of the trauma, as in the journey for Carol. Sometimes I might see just the soul part at a certain age in nonordinary reality, as was the case with Susan. Often I hear orders from my power animal: "Go get the four-year-old." The information always comes differently, and I can always ask for more if I need it.

When Jackie came to me for a soul retrieval, she said she struggled with a lack of self-confidence. As I began my journey, I felt the familiar tug on my solar plexus drawing me to the Upper World. In the far reaches of the darkness I found Jackie at the age of thirty-three, looking very forlorn. "Jackie, what has happened?" I asked. "My husband left me for another woman," she replied. Knowing what I do about soul loss, I suspected that a pattern had started at an earlier age that set up the problematic theme in Jackie's life. So I called out to my power animal at this point, "Show me where it all began." Holding hands, the adult Jackie and I flew back in time and space through the darkness to a scene in a classroom where a young Jackie was sitting very red-faced, surrounded by other six-year-olds in first grade. Jackie's teacher was yelling at her, "Jackie, you are lazy, and you daydream too much. You will never amount to anything in life!" Devastated and humiliated, Jackie's soul left the room, taking her imagination and creativity with her. The part of Jackie that was left kept hearing her teacher's words reverberating in her head. This incident, so long before, was where it all began—Jackie's lifelong struggle for self-esteem.

MULTIPLE SOUL PARTS

In your reading so far, you have learned that most of us have more than one part of ourselves missing. We have experienced a series of traumas at different periods in our lives, causing many pieces of our essence to leave. How many parts can we lose? That really depends on the individual and his or her history. I have found that there must be at least as many parts left in ordinary reality as there are in nonordinary reality. People cannot function if they are more out of their bodies than in.

During most of my soul retrievals, I retrieve as many as three to six parts at one time. In one soul retrieval with Jerry, I found a part of him that left at age five when he fell off his bicycle, one that left at age fourteen during an appendicitis operation, and another that left at age nineteen while he was in Vietnam.

As I mentioned earlier, soul parts can help me while I do my work. I worked with Sherry, who experienced soul loss during the breakup of her marriage at age twenty-eight. She also lost her soul at age four when she felt abandoned as her own parents divorced. I found the four-year-old Sherry, still in her room in the Middle World, trembling with fear. The twenty-eight-year-old part was with me, and she gently picked up the four-year-old and held her to her heart, cradling her, speaking words of comfort and love. She wiped the tears from the child's eyes and kissed her. The words of love and physical comfort brought a smile to brighten up the little girl. A happy duo returned to the forty-four-year-old client lying on my floor waiting to reunite with her lost essence.

When Lois's stubborn thirteen-year-old didn't want to return to ordinary reality with me, her spunky five-year-old was the one to convince the older soul part to go along with us. Witnessing the compassion and comforting shown by stronger parts to scared, fragile, and disappointed parts is always a moving experience for me.

Multiple soul loss might follow a theme. Leslie's soul loss occurred at ages three, sixteen, and twenty-eight, all at times when she felt her freedom and independence being threatened. Kevin's thread of souls scattered in nonordinary reality was caused by feelings of abandonment.

One can return only a certain number of soul parts at one time. The reason for this is simple. When the soul returns, it comes back with all the pain it experienced on leaving. The memories surrounding the trauma often take a while to return. I don't want to overwhelm a person with too many memories of physical and/or emotional pain. The way I know how many parts to bring back is by following directions from my power animal, whose judgment I trust implicitly. When he says, "That's enough for now," my search ends.

Integration of the returned soul parts takes some time. I ask my clients to wait a few months before deciding whether they want another soul retrieval. In the chapter on life after soul retrieval, I will speak more about this issue of integration, but needless to say, depending on the trauma and on the person's emotional and physical health, the period of integration varies considerably.

How do I return the retrieved souls to people? In nonordinary reality I have found many soul parts that might be waiting in my crystal, or might be holding hands with each other and me to form a chain, or maybe riding on the back of a power animal who volunteers to help. My next job is to bring these parts back from nonordinary reality to ordinary reality by visualizing and feeling them reentering with me. I slowly and firmly pull them to my heart, then I physically get up and kneel next to my client. I cup my hands over my client's "heart center" and deliberately blow the soul parts through my hands into the body, visualizing them entering into the entire body. Next, I help my client sit up, and I

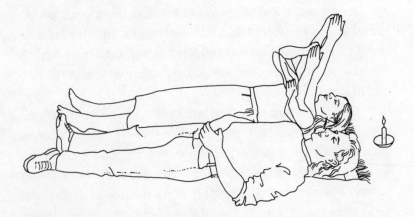

Bringing the Soul into Ordinary Reality

blow the parts into the crown of the head, again visualizing the parts going through the body. Throughout this entire process I maintain some sort of physical contact. I shake my rattle around my clients four times to "seal them up" and then look directly into their eyes and say, "Welcome home."

When I share my experiences with my clients I remind them that I don't know if the information I received was literal or metaphorical, so they must decide what is relevant for them. As I worked with Robert, for example, my intention to find his soul took me to the Lower World, where I saw him as a nine-year-old drowning in the ocean. When I shared this with Robert, he responded that he felt he was "drowning" emotionally rather than physically. Because the information in journeys often comes metaphorically, I am careful not to report my experiences as literal, although they sometimes are. Sharing my experience and allowing the client to sort through the information is a wonderful way to give the client back his or her power without my forcing any interpretation.

As I mentioned earlier in chapter 2, *I will not report a scene of sexual abuse unless I know that my client is already aware of the abuse.*

Blowing in the Soul

I believe it would be highly unethical to do this. So with Steven I reported, "I saw something traumatic that happened to you at the age of seven. Do you have any memory of this?" When he told me he was abused by his uncle, I then went on to fill in the details that were so validating to him. Another client, Karen, had no memory of age four; therefore, I did not share what I saw on my journey. A few weeks later Karen called me to talk about memories of sexual abuse that were coming forth. I then shared with her what I had seen on my journey.

People retrieve memories according to their own inherent timing. I feel it's very important to trust the person's own being to let memories come up when it is the right time and place. Some memories come up during daily activities, and some reveal themselves in dreams. I trust the client's inherent intelligence in these matters.

After sharing my journeys with my clients, I want to give them a few minutes to experience what it feels like to be home.

Blowing in the Soul

I play a wonderful instrument called a Tibetan bowl, which puts out a continuous calming tone. I instruct my clients to lie back down, listen to the sound of the bowl, and simply experience themselves, feeling what it is like to be whole and home again.

At this point our session ends. I give my clients a gift of a stone or crystal so that they can always remember this experience. I also ask them to go to a place in nature, leave an offering or gift, and give thanks for their lives. In a journey a few years ago I was told, "The Earth wants her children home, and She wants them home now." Soul retrieval is such a powerful way to bring people back to their bodies, the Earth, and home again.

AN EXERCISE IN INTENTION AND TRUST

In my workshops I repeatedly emphasize that the keys to healing are intention and trust. I suggest that you might want to think about times in your own life when you brought to yourself something you wanted by focusing clearly on what you were calling to yourself and believing it would come. In other words, you expressed intention and trust. Here is a simple exercise, a good place to begin.

Think about something simple that you would like to manifest. Be realistic about what you're asking for. Set your intention. Write down in one sentence what you want. Observe your beliefs about whether you think it can happen. Take a leap of faith, and trust that it can. Observe how your intention helps you create the actions needed to draw you closer to what you desire.

CHAPTER 5

CLASSICAL EXAMPLES OF SOUL RETRIEVAL

*The only thing of value in a man is the soul. That is
why it is the soul that is given everlasting life, either
in the Land of the Sky or in the Underworld. The soul
is man's greatest power, it is the soul that makes us
human, but how it does so we do not know. Our
flesh and blood, our body, is nothing but an
envelope about our vital power.*
—*Intinilik, an Utkahikjaling Eskimo*

Literature on soul retrieval shows that these ceremonies were practiced all around the world. According to Mircea Eliade and Michael Harner, shamans in many parts of the world undertook ecstatic journeys in search of the soul. I have read about soul loss and/or soul retrieval in Siberia, Central Asia, Indonesia, China, India, North and South America, the Philippines, Northwest Africa, New Guinea, Melanesia, and Australia. Soul retrieval ceremonies vary among cultures. Some of the following examples are not necessarily shamanic in nature; nonetheless they are ceremonies that demonstrate how soul retrieval has been dealt with by other cultures.

In *The Way of the Animal Powers,* Joseph Campbell describes a story of a soul retrieval that also shows the significance of the shaman's drum.

Undoubtedly the most important, as well as most characteristic, of all these Malo-Atlaic features is the drum. The shaman rides on his drum; and the Buriat or Irkutsk declare that by virtue of the power of his originally double-headed drum, their first shaman, Moyan-kara, could bring back souls even from the dead.

Erlen Khan, the Lord of the Dead, complained to the great god Tengri, on high, that because of Moyan-kara he was no longer able to hold the souls brought to him by his messengers; and so Tengri himself determined to make trial of the shaman with a test. He took possession of the soul of a certain man, slipped it into a bottle, and then, sitting with the bottle in hand, his thumb covering its opening, he waited to see what the mighty Buriat would do.

The man whose soul had been taken fell ill, and his family sent for Moyan-kara. The shaman immediately recognized that the soul of the man had been taken, and, riding on his wonderful drum, he searched the forests, the waters, the mountain gorges, indeed the earth, and then descended to the Underworld. The soul being nowhere in any of these, there remained but one domain to be searched: High Heaven. So, sitting on his drum, he flew aloft, and he cruised to the heavens for some time before noticing that the radiant High God was sitting there with a bottle in his hand, over the top of which the ball of his thumb was pressed. Studying the circumstance, Moyan-kara perceived that within the bottle was the very soul he had come to retrieve. So he transformed himself into a wasp, flew at the god, and gave him such a hot sting on the forehead that his thumb jerked from the opening and the soul escaped. The next thing Tengri knew was

that the shaman, together with his prize, was on his drum again,
sailing back to earth. He reached for a thunderbolt, let it fly, and
the drum was split in half, and that is why shaman drums today
have but one head.[1]

Mircea Eliade writes of soul retrieval among the Sea Dyak, of
Borneo:

The Sea Dyak shaman is called manang. *Quartz crystals that*
are considered "stones of light," as well as other magical objects,
are used by this manang to help find the soul of a patient. The
shaman uses a seance to cure illness due to the flight of the
soul. This seance takes place at night. First, the patient's body is
rubbed with stones while an audience sings monotonous tones
and the shaman dances until exhaustion. Once the shaman falls
to the ground, a blanket is thrown over him or her, and the
shaman begins to journey to find the lost soul. The audience
waits. The manang searches for the soul in the Underworld and
when he or she captures it, the manang rises quickly, holding the
part in his or her hand, and then replaces the soul through the
patient's skull.[2]

In *Borderlines*, Charles Nicholl describes soul loss and a
modern-day soul retrieval in Thailand. He was crossing a river in
Thailand, swimming to Laos with a Thai woman named Katai,
when they got caught in the current. This was a very traumatic experience for Katai. Later she explained to him about *khwan hai*—
the loss of her spirit. She explained, "The spirit inside us we call
'khwan.' The 'khwan' is something we might lose many times in
our life. When you are sick, or when you have the big shock,
when this happens we say 'Khwan Khwaen,' which means that
your 'khwan' is hanging above you." She goes on to say: "You
might lose your 'khwan' at some great change in your life, like you
get married, or have a baby, or when someone dies who you love

very much. The 'khwan' is what flies away from us. We call it the butterfly soul, it flies from us so easy."

Katai believed that the river took away her *khwan*, leaving her sad and empty. She felt her grandfather's death, which had occurred a while back, also caused problems with her *khwan*.

She told Charles Nicholl that she had to find someone to perform the *bai see soo khwan*, a ceremony to call back the *khwan*. A *mau khwan* was the specialist in *khwan* ceremonies. The ceremony would cost a lot of money (about thirty dollars), and Charles Nicholl remarked about this. Her response was, "It would be worth it at twice the price. It's like paying for an operation when you're sick. Whatever it costs it has to be done."

Unfortunately, the *mau khwan* was out of town, but Katai was referred to a *prahm*—a spirit man. He was versed in various ceremonies.

Many items were prepared for the offering as well as decorations for the *sao khwan*. Flowers were arranged in bunches and wrapped in a banana leaf. Each leaf was polished to give it a sheen. The flowers were for the *pha khwan*, a tiered, conical structure set on a silver-gilt dish, the holder for the offerings made to entice the *khwan* back. Besides the flowers there were two boiled chickens; a half bottle of whiskey; sweetmeats of sticky rice, sugar cane, and candied marrow; quids of miang; betel leaves and areca nuts; pink birthday candles; and a range of small token gifts—a bracelet, a wristwatch, and a cup for whiskey. Charles Nicholl reacted to these offerings, noting, "There is something very charming about this characterization of the 'khwan' as a flighty, childish creature, won back by these baubles and bonbons laid out for it."

The ceremony proceeded with the spirit man chanting in both Pali and Burmese. One part of his chant was speaking to the thirty-two mini-*khwan*, each a part of the *khwan* that lives in different parts of the body. He spoke to the river spirits and mentioned "Lady Coconut Flower," a kind of wood nymph Katai liked. Then he invoked Katai's *khwan*. His words were, "Come, O 'khwan.' Let not the 'khwan' of the head be discouraged, nor any of the 32 'khwan' of the young girl's body. You may return here safely. Be content. Look, we have prepared a feast for you. We have laid out pretty robes for you to wear, a mirror for you to see yourself, though we cannot see you. We have prepared a splendid feast for you." He went on to each of the offerings. This all went on for about fifteen minutes. Katai was kneeling with her head bowed, her right hand touching the *pha khwan*. The spirit man stopped chanting, and all the participants sat in silence for a couple of minutes.

Then the spirit man nodded and everyone relaxed. During the silence Katai's *khwan* returned, enticed back by the spirit man's chanting and the offerings. Katai's *khwan* came to the *pha khwan;* her *khwan* was not yet in Katai.

The ceremony continued. Katai's hands were dabbed with water from the flowers. Food was given to her to encourage her *khwan* on the last leg of its return. Some of the words used during this time were, "Come, O 'khwan,' feed at her hand. Let her be strong and daring, let her be free of illness, let her open her palms and gain what she wants. Come feed."

Finally an "auspicious thread" was used to seal in Katai's returned *khwan*. This thread is a length of string that has been blessed and then tied around the wrist. The string ties in luck, health, and happiness, which seals in the *khwan*. The ceremony was now complete.[3]

The Circle

Hands
Who listened
  to silence
and spoke
  to darkness
    only a whisper
or was it, to the lost wraith, water
mumbling underground.
Same thing. No.
  Don't move.
    No sound.

But
  a spark
    in closed eyes.
Sun burning
Sky reeling
  in a long forgotten land
No sound
  but the heartbeat
    of the buried sea
calling: Listen
Listen. Some one breathes
  the lost name

Then clearly, in the mossy stillness, sings
  Dear heart,
    come home.

—Diana Rowan

CHAPTER 6

COMMUNITY

*We must, however, reflect on what is happening. It is
an urgent matter, especially for those of us who still
live in a meaningful, even a numinous, earth community. We have not spoken. Nor even have we seen
clearly what is happening. The issue goes far beyond
economics, or commerce, or poetics, or an evening of
pleasantries as we look out over a scenic view.
Something is happening beyond all this. We are losing splendid and intimate modes of divine presence.
We are, perhaps, losing ourselves.*
—Thomas Berry, The Dream of the Earth

*I suggest that each person reading this book begin to create a sense
of group support. To do this simply, find one person with whom you
can share some of the concepts you are reading about in* Soul Retrieval.
*You do not have to explain everything, but take at least one idea that
intrigues you and discuss it with a friend. That simple act of sharing
takes you from a solo journey to that healing process that comes from
another's caring.*

*I*n ancient times, small communities were central to human life.
These tribal societies, acting as a single organism, fostered interde-
pendence among all members. Based on my study of shamanism,

I believe the health and healing of each member of the community was the responsibility of the entire community. Every individual had tremendous support in the emotional, spiritual, and physical healing process.

As humans evolved and developed more sophisticated technology, communities gave way to cities, with their crowding, anonymity, and indifference. We moved from tribal societies to a culture in which families took the place of the community. As society became more mobile, family clans broke into smaller and more isolated units, down to the "nuclear family." Even now the nuclear family is dissolving into individual members who live separately.

I bring this up because the disintegration of community into ever more discrete units of human interaction has a dramatic effect on soul loss. I feel strongly that the sense of community has an important influence on soul retrieval work. Not only do many of us today have no community support to draw on, but also the isolation many of us feel is itself a major cause of soul loss.

Let me explain. In researching how shamans traditionally dealt with soul retrievals, I found that a crucial element in the ceremony was the community's participation. Eliade's *Shamanism: Archaic Techniques of Ecstasy* is filled with accounts of shamans of different cultures calling back the soul. He describes rituals and ceremonies surrounding soul loss and retrieval from Central and North Asia, North and South America, Indo-European societies, and Tibet, China, and other parts of the Far East. Looking at some of these simple ceremonies shows us the integral place of community and the importance of having someone "waiting" for the return of the patient's soul.

In Central Asia, for example, Eliade describes how the Teleut shaman "calls back the soul of the sick child in these words: 'Come back to your country! . . . to the yurt, by the bright fire! . . . Come back to your father . . . to your mother.'"

A more elaborate ritual is performed by the Buryat shaman of Central Asia, who seats himself on a rug beside the patient. The shaman is surrounded by many objects. For example, an arrow is tied with red silk thread that extends from the arrow's point, through the open door of the yurt, to a birch tree outside. The soul of the patient can return along this thread.

The Buryat also believe that a horse can perceive the return of the soul; the horse will begin to quiver as the soul returns. A horse is left out at the birch tree near where the red silk thread is tied, and someone holds the horse. Inside the yurt a table is set up with cakes, tarasun, brandy, and tobacco. The age of the patient determines the guests who will be invited to the seance. Children are invited to a seance for a child; grown men come to a seance for an adult; and older people are invited to the seance if the patient is elderly. The Buryat shaman searches for the patient's soul. But before the search, he starts with an invocation. "Your father is A, your mother B, your own name is C. Where are you lingering, whither have you gone? . . . Sad sit those in the yurt." The people who are present begin to cry, and the shaman speaks of the grief and sadness. "Your wife and your dear children, so unexpectedly orphaned, call you hopelessly weeping and wailing, and cry to you, 'Father, where are you?' Hear and have pity on them, come back to them. . . . Your herd of countless horses longs for you, whinnying loudly and crying pitifully, 'Where art thou, our master? Come back to us.'"[1]

WHO IS WAITING?

In Eliade's accounts we see two things: first, a shaman was needed to intercede in the spiritual realm for the client's healing, and second, whether it was the father, the mother, people in the yurt, or the community in general, someone was waiting for the soul's return. This correlates with what I have found in my own work. When I met with Carol one year after our session, I asked her what the most important aspect of the soul retrieval had been for her. She replied that the most profound part of the experience was that someone cared enough about her to search for and retrieve her lost soul. The concern of a client's support system is so important in the healing process. I think that attempting soul retrievals for oneself may not work because there is no community to welcome the soul home.

Here a controversy arises, because much of the focus of alternative therapies has been in the direction of self-healing. It is clear to me that soul retrieval is not a self-help technique. As in classic shamanism, it is important for one person, the shaman, to intervene in the spiritual realms for the client. And what I have discovered in my own work is the great power derived from another person's witnessing the return of the soul and welcoming it back. Naturally, there are exceptions. Occasionally I receive letters from people telling me of miraculous and spontaneous soul retrievals that occur in their own shamanic journeys. These, too, have precedents in classical shamanism, where accounts of miraculous healings exist but do not seem to be the norm.

I am not saying that self-healing doesn't work. Obviously it does, in some cases. However, a balance is needed. I do teach people to journey in order to heal themselves and make progress in their lives. But in many cases, of which soul retrieval is but one example, we must invoke the traditional role of the shaman to provide what the clients can't provide for themselves. The client's role begins after the soul retrieval. The soul retrieval is where the work really begins.

The problems we have as a society today—social injustice, crime, environmental problems—require that we move out of our lives of isolation and band together, acting communally to find solutions that extend beyond the scope of the problems. Without discarding the concept of self-healing, we must recognize the need for a healing process of power and love that involves the support of others.

I am so convinced of the importance of community to the success in the work of soul retrieval that in my initial interview with a client, I ask for information about the person's support system. I want to know that there is someone in that person's life who honestly cares if he or she comes back home. That person may be a therapist, a lover, a friend, or a family member. Several of my students who use this process in their own practices require each client to bring a friend. Not only does the friend add to the power of the process, he or she shares in the celebration once it is over.

MODERN-DAY STRESSES

But what happens when the community system fails? Recently, the United States Surgeon General reported a sobering statistic: emotional and/or physical abuse occurs in one out of every four families. One can safely assume that children from these families are indeed traumatized. This means that the children in 25 percent of American families face the possibility of soul loss—the loss of their essence and vitality—due to everyday family life. Has the evolution from community and tribal societies to nuclear families put too much pressure on us as adults to tolerate and endure the demands of parenting, especially within the increasing stress of living in contemporary society?

Just as soul loss can occur within families, it can also take place as those family units dissolve through separation and divorce. Children can be devastated by the disintegration of their security and community—their family. The soul loss that results from the child's feelings of abandonment can be quite dramatic.

John came to me for a soul retrieval. He complained of an inability to stay in relationships and constantly battled with the issues of trust and intimacy.

I begin my journey and meet my power animal. My intention is to see whether I can find any lost parts of John that would be helpful in helping him deal with his issues. My power animal takes me to a house in the Middle World. I look around the brightly colored living room. There is a tapestry-covered couch and two Victorian-style chairs. My attention is drawn to loud shouting coming from the far end of the room. At the bottom of a staircase is John's father, shouting at his mother that he is leaving. On the floor of the living room sits four-year-old John, looking panic-stricken. His father slams out of the house; his mother slams a door upstairs; and John's soul flees in terror from the experience. With his father's leaving, John's normal family life shatters, and the abandonment he feels is just too much to endure.

I speak with the soul part of John, assuring him that John is waiting in ordinary reality and will take care of him. The four-year-old sees that he is the part of John that knows how to trust and agrees to return home again.

Not only might being in community take the pressure off of raising children, it might also take some of the pressure off of being in relationships. Often in our relationships we put all our needs on our partner, which is quite unrealistic. No one person can meet all our needs. Having friends or an extended family who deeply care about us might help solve this problem.

RITES OF PASSAGE

Besides providing a safe place for raising children, communities also celebrated important rites of passage and rituals for all their members. Many of these functions have been lost in modern society, and their absence can contribute to soul loss in some individuals.

Carl Jung states, "For thousands of years rites of initiation have been teaching rebirth from the spirit, yet man has forgotten the meaning of divine initiatory procreation in our times. This forgetfulness causes him to suffer a loss of soul, a condition that sadly is everywhere present today." Robert Francis Johnson, a psychotherapist, continues by saying, "This loss of soul Jung speaks of is manifested in our culture by the crises we are all facing (increased drug use, violence, moral and emotional numbness) and our attempt to solve moral and spiritual questions by electing wounded leaders who promise economic answers."[2]

The ritual of childbirth has changed dramatically, for example. In older societies, a woman was surrounded and supported by women friends and relatives during labor and birth. That custom has been replaced by the isolation of modern hospital technology. One practice in particular, that of anesthetizing mothers to ease their pain, has had repercussions for their babies. In my journeys I have seen that children whose mothers were drugged during labor often came into the world disoriented. In working with one man, I saw in my journey that his soul had floated away like a balloon at the time of his birth. Throughout his life he had experienced a debilitating sense of disorientation.

Many women are now choosing to give birth to their children more naturally. Once again, the sacredness of bringing life onto this earth is affirmed. When such births take place at home or at least in a birthing room, the souls being born can be welcomed with warmth and celebration by a waiting community. How different that is from the impersonality of a delivery in an efficient but cold hospital room!

Soul loss also occurs frequently in girls at the onset of puberty. Our society has not preserved the rites of passage common in other cultures. A large percentage of the women I see lost a piece of their essence at the onset of menstruation. They were confused and overwhelmed by natural physiological changes and could not

Soul Retrieval

understand the transition from young girl to sensual, life-giving woman. Frightened, a part of the essence split off and departed. This fear and confusion can be magnified if the woman has suffered any kind of sexual abuse as a child. Whenever soul loss happens at menarche, we see a woman who cannot embrace her feminine power. She may choose to inhibit her sexuality, perhaps because the feelings are too overwhelming or because she fears men. Or she may become anorexic or bulemic because the body of a mature woman is threatening to her. However she responds, she cuts herself off from her own goddess nature, and this fragmentation frequently leads to depression or anger.

In my work with men I often see soul loss occurring in the teen years. The social and peer pressure of moving from boy to social male is often overwhelming. I often see it manifest in the confusion about how to act socially toward girls turning to women. It is during this time of awkwardness in approaching women and dealing with dating that the soul often leaves.

I have seen that the effects of war upon young men lead to their soul loss. Participating in the taking of life, fearing the loss of one's own life, feeling intense pain—all these are more than enough to make a part of the soul depart in search of more comforting surroundings.

Vietnam veterans are a case in point. In contrast to the survivors of other wars, they found no community waiting to welcome them home, a reality that still pains many veterans today and contributes to even greater soul loss. In fact, this group of traumatized individuals constitutes one of the most tragic examples of soul loss we see today. The potential benefit of soul retrieval work among Vietnam veterans is high, as long as a supportive community exists to help them integrate their lost parts.

Many people in our society have turned to organized religion to replace the community of tribes and clans. There must be a great sense of comfort gained from filing into a sacred place to pray together with a group of people. In churches and temples, children's classes and social groups have fostered a sense of belonging among members. Perhaps the time has come to go beyond this model—to go beyond the community that meets once a week to help us deal with our sins. If we are truly to inhabit the earth, I feel that our current communities, whether they be religious, political, or social, must continue to stress the celebration and sacredness of life. What a quality we are ignoring! We have gotten so caught up in survival and in redeeming ourselves from sin that we have forgotten celebration. A celebration of life that comes from joining in partnership to share skills and knowledge, to truly create a way of living that honors life and nature, would help us move out of a world of disease and problems and achieve balance.

My vision is to support and honor the beauty of life and to work together with others—to celebrate the "highs" and resolve the challenge of the "lows" in a truly supportive way. I ask each one of you to stretch your imagination to see yourself living in a truly nurturing society. See it in all its details; give it a story; feel it, hear it, smell it, become it.

USING THE CIRCLE

In a recent workshop I agreed to do a soul retrieval for a man for whom I felt great empathy. I had listened to the story of how, in the country in which he lived, he had little support for what he was doing. Spiritual work was immediately classified by his community as sorcery, and he was aware that his life was in danger.

The focus of the workshop was soul retrieval training; there were thirty-eight participants. During some group drumming and rattling at the beginning of the day, I heard the voice of one of my teachers, the Goddess Innana, whisper to me, "Be careful." I shuddered. Innana is not usually interested in my soul retrieval work, and her presence was a very serious omen to me.

Later that day I began my work with Ailo. I wanted deeply to help my friend, to send him home feeling whole and energized to meet his challenges. I felt great pressure and had twinges of performance anxiety. Soon thirty-eight people were going to be observing my work. I also felt fear from the warning I had received that morning.

I asked everyone to form a circle, holding hands. "Breathe deeply and slowly, raising your own energy as well as the whole circle's energy. Remember the connection we have with all life. Remember our connection with other circles in nature—the moon, the sun, the earth, the drum." I felt life force pumping through me, coming in through the person on my right, going out to the person on my left.

I felt my blood pulsating through every vein of my body and a tremendous amount of heat rising up through me, in my solar plexus and my arms, into my face. I felt very big. I was drawing from the power of the circle and was giving back to it at the same time.

I then began to speak to all in the room, participants of the circle as well as to the spirits. "Ailo has asked for help in coming back home. Mother, please help me bring your son home where he can take his rightful place on earth—to enjoy all the pleasures of being alive."

To Ailo I said, "Ailo, this circle is for you. Anxiously, each and every person here is waiting for you, waiting for you to come home."

I then asked Ailo to leave the circle with me and enter the middle. He lay down on my rug. There was a candle at his head, the only light in the room. I knelt next to him, picked up my rattle, and began to sing my song. There was so much more power flowing through my body than when I work alone. I was aware of the energy of the circle supporting me. The power was over-whelming me. I felt so big! I also was beginning to feel very light-headed. I knew it was time to begin. I no longer knew who I was; I was overtaken by the force of power going through me. I lay down next to Ailo, touching him. This was the signal for the drummer to drum loudly in a moderately fast and steady beat.

> *Repeating my intention, I am drawn down, down, down into the Lower World. Darkness surrounds me, and I cannot see. Why can't I see? Someone is trying to stop me from seeing. I know I am being watched. I scream into the universe for help. My power animal appears. He rarely takes conditions very seriously and has a wonderful sense of humor. He looks at me and asks, "What are you getting so excited about?" I reply, "I can't see." He reaches into his pocket and takes out a flashlight, which he proceeds to turn on for me. He hands it to me, and I take it from him. I am in a very dark place, but with the light of the flashlight I start to see the outline of a box. I am aware of a very imposing presence with me, and then Innana appears. This is unusual, because she never appears in my journeys for another person. She escorts me to this strong steel box. I know the dark, powerful presence cannot compare to the power of Innana and my guardian. I feel safe. I also am very aware of the power of the circle around me.*

> *I open the box, and there is the soul of Ailo. With the lid lifted, Ailo can uncurl himself, and he steps out, looking quite dazed. His soul had been stolen by someone who was jealous of his power and who didn't want to see him succeed in his work.*

> *With all the power from the helping spirits and that of the circle I feel the dark presence flee. The Lower World room I'm in slowly lights up. Although the light is dim, I can see better. The room is square, and the ceiling, walls, and floor are cold, packed, brown dirt. Innana says, "Tell Ailo as long as he continues to do work that promotes and supports life on earth and in all the mother's*

children, that he has nothing to fear." I repeat those words to Ailo and ask him if he understands. He says yes. I ask him if he wants to return with me, and he again responds yes. Innana disappears. I ask my power animal if there are more parts out there. He says there are.

The three of us are then drawn to the Middle World to another time and place when Ailo was four or five years old. He has on a red-and-white wool cap and gloves, and he is in the snow. A woman is bending over, yelling something at him. Ailo feels unloved and uncared for. My power animal says that a theme for Ailo in his life is feeling isolated and as though he doesn't fit in. He is seeking a family. I ask Ailo if he will come with us. He goes into the arms of the adult Ailo.

Our mission takes us up into the stars to still another part of Ailo, one that is twenty-eight years old. He tells me that he left due to a broken heart. He also agrees to come back with us. The three souls hug one another, and we all hold on together.

Strongly pulling the souls from nonordinary reality into ordinary reality, I quickly blow them all into the body of my client. I rattle around Ailo to seal him up and welcome him home. We hear voices coming from the community, echoing from each person, "Welcome home, Ailo!" I report my journey to Ailo and the community. Ailo explains the synchronicities and fills in the details of each soul's story.

He asks me if he can do a thank-you dance. His dance becomes increasingly ecstatic until finally he drops to the floor. I put my hand on his shoulder, and he says, "I'm home."

For me as a shamanic practitioner, the power that came from this circle added immensely to my sense of the work. For Ailo, the community provided the family he was waiting for. It was quite a moving experience. My only wish is that I could have such a circle at each of my soul retrieval sessions, but there are also other ways to network with others and create support. We all have friends with whom we can share our experiences; when a client brings a friend to a soul retrieval, we then have an instant community.

I become part of the client's community during and after the soul retrieval. A therapist or bodyworker or someone else in the helping profession can be there for support, as well. Our task now is to form intentional communities. All of us need people to network with to share our joys and sorrows and help us feel that we are not so alone and will not be abandoned. My experience has been that people who have soul retrievals find that there are many people in their lives with whom they can celebrate their homecoming.

In chapter 5 I relayed the story of Katai and her soul retrieval. At a later date Charles Nicholl went to visit Katai, and they spoke of the ceremony. Katai said, "You were there when I got back my spirit. You helped get it back."

Charles replied, "I did nothing."

Katai responded, "You were there, Charlie. Being there was enough."[3]

In a circle of friends

The circle is singing
The drum is starting
The shaman is journeying
The shaman is raising up

She brought my soul
back from far away,
with energy for me,
knowledge for me.

A soul-thief unmasked.

Circle, I sing to you.
Sun, I dance to you.
Soul, I laugh and cry
to welcome you Home.

—Ailo Gaup

CHAPTER 7

WHEN SOULS HAVE BEEN STOLEN

*A Taulipang myth relates the search for the soul of a
child that the moon had carried off and hidden
under a pot; the shaman goes up to the moon
and, after many adventures, finds the
pot and frees the child's soul.*
—*Mircea Eliade,* Shamanism:
Archaic Techniques of Ecstasy

A serious phenomenon I see when searching for souls is that
sometimes a soul has actually been stolen by another person. I often hear incest survivors who know nothing about shamanism
say, "My father stole my soul," or "My uncle stole my soul."
Similarly, people who have been caught in abusive relationships
frequently claim, "My lover stole my soul."

For lack of a better word in the English language, I use the
word *thief* for a person who steals a soul. But I use this word
without judgment or blame. Soul stealing is often done out of ignorance rather than intent to harm. Soul theft is a hard concept
for many of us to grasp. Why would someone commit what
amounts to grand larceny on a human level? How can we explain this? And how can we take a compassionate stance on the
issue of soul stealing?

In most cases of soul stealing the thief is also a victim of soul theft. Through contemporary psychology, we have discovered that people who abuse usually were abused themselves. Likewise, soul stealing is generational; therefore, doing a soul retrieval for a person whose soul has been stolen may end family karma. Bringing back the soul and educating the client about the concept of soul theft and loss prevents this behavior from being passed down to future generations.

But why steal another person's soul? One reason is power. The thief might envy the person's power and might attempt to take that power for personal use, putting the thief in the position of power over the victim. It is sad but all too common for a person who feels powerless to deal with this feeling by moving into a power-over stance. For example, if a father feels powerless because he's unable to create wholeness in his own life, he might move into stealing the soul of his young, defenseless child by raping or beating the child or his wife. In this way he is saying, "I am more powerful than you." Yet he is creating a false sense of self.

In our society the word *power* is understood by most of us as *power over* another person. The two words seem to go together. Because people generally have no concept of what personal power means, most of my clients, especially women, have no understanding of how to avoid giving their personal power away to another person. This lack of understanding of power goes hand in hand with soul stealing. A person who is willing to give away his or her personal power to another becomes vulnerable to soul theft. Children, who usually don't know how to protect themselves physically, are especially susceptible to having their souls stolen.

Another reason for soul stealing is the mistaken belief that one person's essence, vitality, and power can be used by someone else. For example, I worked with a woman whose soul was stolen at the age of three months by her mother. Her mother saw such light and energy in the baby that she felt that if she could have just a part of this child, it would restore her own vitality. A common pattern I see is that clients who had a part of their souls taken at an early age tend to be chronically ill as children. They lose part of their vitality and therefore don't have the power or the will to fight off illness. After the soul retrieval it's not unusual for a client to rattle off a long list of childhood illnesses.

The same scene appears repeatedly in my journeys. To protect themselves in the psychic battle with a parent, children surrender their will. What I see is a child who has given up—hunched over, turned in, and despondent. The effects of soul theft at an early age are manifested similarly in these clients as adults. Often, through these life experiences, they have become very protective of their energy and vitality and look very "pulled in." It's almost as if they have a need to hide their "light" or vitality so that no one will try to take it away again. I also find that a common complaint among these clients is a lack of hope and will in their lives.

The belief that we can use another person's light, power, energy, or essence for our own good is a misunderstanding. Certainly, you can reflect an individual's light and power, but you cannot use them as a source of your own energy. Each one of us must reach inside ourselves to find our own power sources.

RESTORING ANGELA'S LIGHT

When Angela came to see me for a soul retrieval, she complained that she was always withdrawn. She didn't feel able to take a stand in the world or to get ahead by demonstrating her talents. She also felt that she had issues of abandonment to work through. Her history revealed that at age four, she had been hospitalized with pneumonia. From what Angela now knew of psychology, she suspected she was carrying around feelings of abandonment from that time. She assumed she must have felt abandoned and scarred by the separation from her parents.

I begin my journey by going to the Lower World—through my tree trunk, into my tunnel, and out into the pine forest where my power animal resides. I tell him about Angela and ask him if there is any information or anything I can do that will be helpful to her.

Together we move through time and space to the Middle World. A white house with a picket fence stands before us. We open the gate and go through the front door, wandering through the living room, which is cluttered with lots of things. As we walk through, I can smell something sweet baking in the oven. It is a nice, sunny afternoon, and lots of light streams through the windows.

I follow the smell into the kitchen, my power animal walking beside me. To one seeing with ordinary vision, the kitchen scene that I observe is that of a happy bond between mother and daughter. There is three- or four-year-old Angela with her blond curls and green dress on the floor playing with her stuffed bear. Angela's mom is lovingly mixing cookie batter. But looking with the strong eye, a psychic battle is going on. Angela's mother, worn out by the drudgery of cooking, cleaning, and raising children, is tired and despondent. Angela, by contrast, has such life force and energy, and a strong will.

Angela stubbornly resists her mother's attempt to attach a psychic cord to her, to use some of the child's energy for herself. She loves her mom, but unconsciously she knows her mother wants her life or light. She struggles against her mom, but finally, she can no longer endure. The psychic desire of the adult is too much for this child to withstand.

Angela collapses psychically and lets her soul go to her mother. Again, to an observer with ordinary vision, all things in the kitchen seem the same. To one seeing what is being hidden, Angela is now different: her essence has been taken from her. Soon after this event, Angela becomes ill with pneumonia and fights for her life in the hospital.

I stand in the kitchen observing all that is happening. I go to Angela's mother. She is a nice woman, who looks like a typical mom. She does love Angela. She is not jealous of her child as I sometimes see with parents; she is just exhausted by her life.

I say to her, "Angela needs her soul back." She looks up at me, startled; she has been caught. I keep talking. "Angela cannot lead a healthy, productive life as long as you hold on to her soul. If you really love Angela, please give it back."

She starts to cry and wipes her tears with her stained apron. She says, "I'm sorry. Of course you can have it back." She gives me Angela's soul, and in return I give her a beautiful gold ball that immediately brightens her up. Light essence is exchanged for light essence.

I returned to ordinary reality with Angela's soul and blew it into her. After I welcomed her home, we talked about the experience. What I saw from my journey was how, after losing her soul at age three or four, she had turned inward and become self-protective so that no one else could steal whatever light she had left. And so she associated showing herself, her talents, her light to the world with someone's wanting to take them from her. I explained to Angela that she was now old enough to protect herself without having to hide who she was; she could be whoever she wanted to be. If she felt herself becoming drained in someone else's presence, she could simply visualize herself surrounded by white light, or she could "put" herself into a blue egg that would protect her. (This latter is a technique taught to me by a Chumash medicine woman I met at a gathering in the San Francisco Bay Area many years ago. A group of us were discussing different methods we had for protecting ourselves from other people's energies. This medicine woman shared with us that she visualizes herself into a blue egg. I tried it myself, and for years the method has been serving me well when I feel some outside energy trying to get into my field.)

Another way Angela could protect herself and hold on to her energy and light would be calling her own power animal to her. She decided to learn how to journey for herself. Upon leaving her tunnel in the Lower World, she found a great white bear who told her she would remain with her. The bear encouraged Angela to be herself and open up to let her light and power shine through. She now had the tools she needed to do this in a safe way.

Angela felt that she now needed to nurture this four-year-old part of herself, to let her know she wouldn't be abandoned again and that she could be herself. Though she now felt light and expansive, she began to cry, remembering how hard it had been to protect herself for so many years. Angela now could breathe deeper into her body without its contracting into a fear space; this made her feel free and also a little overwhelmed at the same time.

The night after Angela's soul retrieval session, she called me, feeling troubled. She said that the feelings she was experiencing in her body were not comfortable for her. There was too much energy in her body. I asked her if she felt raw, and she replied that this was exactly how she felt. I explained to her that this was a common experience. For years, out of fear, she had contracted and hadn't let energy pass through her body. To protect herself she had to block her feelings, which cut her off from any life force.

Now she was open, and life force was pulsating through her. It felt raw, she reported, as if her nervous system were on fire. I let her know I felt this was a good sign, and I shared with her the tried-and-true method that I use with myself and others to work through such feelings. I discovered this method on my own years ago when I was running too much energy through my body. I told her just to say the following words to herself: "I ask to get in touch with my higher consciousness. I ask higher consciousness to let in only as much energy as my body can handle at this present time." For Angela, this technique worked within minutes.

Depending on how blocked we have been, we sometimes have to moderate the amount of energy and information coming through. A person's constitution, which is often dependent on diet and physical exercise, determines how much energy he or she can handle. Angela allowed the feeling of being alive to pulsate through her body a little more each week. She was no longer overwhelmed by the feelings but learned how to moderate them. She began to enjoy experiencing the raw power of the earth.

SOUL THEFT AND LOSS

In what other ways can a soul be stolen? In a divorce or breakup of a relationship that is not mutual, the grief-stricken lover might attempt to stay connected by taking part of the ex-lover's soul. But what this does to the other person is it draws from their own life force, leaving a feeling of being drained and interfering with the ability to create new nurturing situations in his or her own life. There is still a connection or cord to the ex-lover and a lack of freedom to create new options, for both concerned.

When a person dies, he or she might be lonely for a loved one left behind. Here again, it is possible for the deceased to take that living person's essence along. The effect of this type of soul loss is the same as that of soul theft by an ex-lover: fatigue and inability to create new, loving relationships. In some cases, the victim even becomes seriously ill in an attempt to join the deceased. The problem here is that in maintaining a connection with the living person, the deceased one is unable to move on in the journey to the light. Both souls are in a state of limbo.

David came to me in extremely poor physical condition. He had Epstein-Barr virus as well as a host of other infections. When he talked about himself, he shared with me that just prior to his falling ill, his girlfriend, Suzanne, had committed suicide.

I did a diagnostic journey to see what would be helpful for David at this time. I again traveled into the Lower World, where I met my power animal and stated the purpose of my journey. My power animal clearly told me that David's soul had been stolen by his girlfriend. I returned from my journey and made the usual preparations for doing a soul retrieval, getting David ready as well as myself.

> As the drumming begins, I state clearly that I am looking for any part of David that will be helpful for him to have back at this time. This intention draws me into nonordinary reality, into the Middle World. I find myself standing in a forest that looks similar to an Eastern forest. I am surrounded by oak trees that have dropped their leaves. The ground is covered with piles of leaves, some still retaining the color of early fall—red, orange, and yellow, with some that have already turned brown—and my feet crunch through them, creating lots of crackling sounds as I walk. My appearance is not discreet because of all the noise I am making. The air is very clean and crisp, and I inhale deeply. I look up, and although there are many clouds in the sky, it is very blue in the background. I love fall and start to get lost in the beauty of my surroundings.
>
> I repeat my intention to focus myself. As I walk, I come to a tree where I see David tied by a rope around the trunk. He looks very forlorn and spiritually beaten. His head hangs down, and his soul shows no vitality. I don't like what I see, and I feel sensations of danger deep in my solar plexus. I yell out in nonordinary reality for my power animal to come and help me. No sooner do I call

than he appears. He is just in time! Suddenly a woman jumps out from behind the tree where she is hiding and lunges at me with her imposing nails aiming for my face. My power animal steps in front of me, creating a force field around us that she can't break through. She repeatedly lunges at the field in anger but keeps being thrown backward into the leaves. Finally, when she is exhausted, we carefully let the field down and walk close to her. She bursts into tears and begins sobbing. She is Suzanne.

"Do you know you are dead?" I ask, and she answers yes. Then I tell her, "I can help you move to a comfortable place if you would like to go with me. But you must release David's soul, or you cannot move on."

"Never," she insists.

This is not going to be easy, I say to myself. I look to my animal for guidance. He says, "Keep talking."

"David is dying back in ordinary reality, because of your keeping his soul captive."

"That's good," she replies. "I want him to die, so he will keep me company here. I want him to stay with me forever."

Soul stealing is so hard to deal with. Although my anger and frustration are rising up inside, overwhelming me, I cannot harm Suzanne. I reach into my pocket and pull out a quartz crystal and hand it to her. She loves the sparkling light, which starts to whirl around and through her. She obviously is soaking it up.

"I can take you to a place where the light shines all the time and will take care of you."

She asks, "How do I get there?"

"Give me back David's soul, and I'll take you there." Suzanne looks at the crystal and then at David and then at me. Seconds go by that seem like hours, and finally she agrees to release David.

I untie David from the tree. He slides to the ground, lying still; his breathing is shallow. I leave him there in the care of my power animal.

I put my arm around Suzanne's and we float upward. We continue to move up and out of this place and travel through space, surrounded by planets and stars. Suddenly we come to a skin membrane, which we break through. Our pace quickens as we continue to rise, going through layer upon layer of clouds. In the distance there is a great blinding light. I know I can go no farther. "Suzanne, go to the light." At this point I push her up, watching her disappear into the all-encompassing golden rays.

I retrace my steps back to where I left David. His condition is critical, and I am reluctant to bring the soul back to David, waiting in ordinary reality.

Finally a tiger appears to me, showing itself to me four times, which I know is a sign that it is volunteering to help David. The tiger goes to the soul of David and infuses him with energy and life. I ask David if he's ready to go home. He nods and then gets onto the back of the tiger. I thank my power animal for his help.

David's soul and the tiger return with me to ordinary reality. Clutching them to my heart, I blow them both into David's heart and then into his crown. After rattling around David to seal him up and welcome him home, I tell him my story.

I explain to David that his lover stole his soul. She did not want to be without him after she chose to take her own life. When people die, they cannot move on to the light while holding onto someone's soul. This action causes them to be bound to the Middle World.

For David the experience of having his soul blown back into his body produced quite an energy rush. He felt like leaving my room and running around outside. His eyes were quite shiny. It always fascinates me how, after every soul retrieval, my clients' eyes get so shiny. A friend of mine who is a doctor explained that this phenomenon is caused by the endorphins being released into the body. With his own soul returned to him, David gradually regained strength and vitality. Within a few months his symptoms of fatigue and the infections disappeared, and he continues to enjoy good health.

David's story is an example of soul stealing as the cause of illness. It is not always the only cause, and shamanic healing work usually needs to continue.

RETRIEVING A STOLEN SOUL

Retrieving a stolen soul is complicated. Typically soul thieves believe that their survival depends on the other person's life force. They are usually not agreeable to returning the soul or are so attached to the person, they won't let the soul go. Yet, in the practice of shamanism, a shaman must act in accordance with the harmony of the universe, which means one cannot do harm to a person who has stolen another person's soul. I have now taught hundreds of people how to retrieve souls. In our journeys we seem to be shown two common ways to retrieve stolen souls.

The first method is reasoning with the thief by explaining how the thief's actions and behavior are causing harm to another person. We often ask them to release the soul in exchange for a gift. A common gift seems to be balls of gold light. Sometimes the practitioner might retrieve a power animal for the thief, a guardian spirit who will then provide a personal source of energy and strength. These techniques usually work well to get a thief to release a captured soul.

When looking shamanically at the thief, one sees that he or she also suffers from soul loss. So a very effective way to deal with this issue is to do a soul retrieval for the thief. Once the thief has personal power and vitality, there is no need to use someone else's.

Another way to get a soul released is to use some form of trickery. For instance, my power animal might distract a thief while I grab the soul. This is one area of working with soul theft that brings up an inner struggle for me. How far do I go to retrieve a soul from a thief? In the practice of shamanism I cannot obliterate or harm a soul thief. The principle of cause and effect holds true for shamans. If I hurt a soul thief in nonordinary reality, that same action might reverberate against me.

But it has been common for shamans to use trickery in dealing with soul theft. Basically what this means is stealing the soul back from the thief. On the one hand, we can say thieves deserve this trickery for stealing what was not theirs in the first place. On the other hand, my knowing that the thief also suffers from soul loss touches my compassionate side.

I was speaking to this issue once in one of my training workshops. A student stopped me to express that she thought I was falling into a psychological trap and that shamans should use whatever means they need to get the soul back, regardless of the patient's or the thief's feelings. Her point is valid, but I believe we must constantly update the ancient techniques to address our current place in human evolution. Consciousness is continually changing. What was psychologically beneficial for a patient hundreds of years ago in Siberia might not be beneficial in the time and culture that we live in today. For this reason, I always attempt a healing on the soul thief, whether I use trickery, love, or negotiation to release the soul to me.

One of my clients, Mary, was going through a very difficult divorce. When I journeyed to diagnose her problem, I saw that there was a tug-of-war going on between her and her estranged husband. This contest was over a light representing Mary's soul.

In nonordinary reality I yelled at Mary to let go. She did, and her husband flew backward with such force that he lost his grip on the light. My power animal then ran in and grabbed it, and we ran off together to return the light to Mary. I then returned to Mary's husband and gave him a gift.

Many clients, upon hearing that someone has stolen their soul, become very concerned about the welfare of the thief, instead of feeling hate. I reassure the client that the thief has been given some form of gift or healing, and whenever I can, I have the person journey to the thief to resolve their unfinished business. The beauty of this method is that both people have what they need to continue on their own life's path or their soul's journey in a clear and empowered way.

SOUL THEFT AND LOVE

Many of us take a part of someone we know so that we can feel connected to them. We must have compassion for ourselves in understanding our need to do this and to find other less destructive means to feel love and connection for another person. In my workshops students frequently come to me and say, "Oh my God, I have my lover's soul. What should I do?" We all must find a way to release those parts and allow people to love us without having to chain them to us. Suggestions on working with this issue are discussed in chapter 11. I truly believe that when we see these behaviors in ourselves it is a gift instead of a curse. In becoming aware of our actions, conscious or unconscious, we can change them.

A controversy that often arises in my training workshops is the concept that there are no unwilling victims or, if you will pardon the cliché, "It takes two to tango." I firmly believe this is true. So what makes someone a willing victim of soul theft? There are many possibilities, and the dynamics are often very complicated.

With children, their psychic defenses simply may not be strong enough to withstand overpowering by another family member, sibling or parent, in the battle for the soul, and they will hand over the soul part in an attempt to survive or because they are fatigued by the struggle. For some children giving the soul part is an attempt to gain or experience love from a family member—part of the soul in exchange for love. When love is not coming in any other way, a child might give in to this abusive bribery to get it.

This happens with adults, too, whether it be in love, friendship, or even in professional relationships. They seem to say, "Here is part of my soul—my essence, my vitality, my power. Now will you love me? Now will you need me? Now will you recognize me?" If we are insecure and don't have a strong sense of self, we often don't realize that there are other ways to have someone love and acknowledge us without our having to sell our souls. After a person has had a soul part taken, the defenses against its being taken again are weaker; thus an individual might fall into a pattern of releasing soul parts to a thief instead of learning techniques of psychic defense. This way of relating contributes to a significant problem in our society—codependency.

The flip side of soul stealing is a truly voluntarily giving of a part of one's soul to another. For example, when a loved one dies, the survivor's soul may try to join the deceased out of grief and love. Or, in a relationship one partner might send a piece of his or her soul to the lover to avoid having to disconnect. In dealing with issues of grief and loss, I often see that part of a client's soul is still with the person who left.

In one case I worked with a divorced woman, Laura, who just couldn't get over the breakup of her marriage. In doing a soul retrieval for Laura, I found myself taking a Middle World journey, during which I discovered a part of Laura's soul was still with her ex-husband because she was so lonely for him. I found that part of her sitting with him in the house they had shared. When I explained to them the condition Laura was in because of the divorce, the fragmented part agreed to return so that Laura could feel whole again and move forward in her life. Laura told me that before the soul retrieval she had felt empty, as if there were a hole inside her, and that as I blew her soul back in, she actually experienced being filled up with her own essence. After the session, Laura began to feel a sense of personal power; that is, energy and the ability to create in her life.

Our goal in doing soul retrievals is to fill people up with their own selves, so they have the energy to create their lives in a meaningful way. Taking another person's soul or giving away one's own does not foster clarity on one's life path.

Codependency is a common issue today; my workshops are filled with people trying to break out of codependent relationships and patterns. I believe that codependency is another way of describing soul loss. To rescue another person or to collude in abusive patterns is to give away one's soul in an attempt to hold onto the relationship. The result is paralyzed, unhappy people.

In *Healing the Shame that Binds You*, John Bradshaw writes that "Co-dependency is a condition where one has no inner life. Happiness is on the outside." He uses the term *toxic shame* and equates it to spiritual bankruptcy, thereby labeling toxic shame a spiritual problem. He goes on to say this causes an alienation of the self from the self, causing it to become "otherated."[1] We then turn to outside sources to fill the void we feel.

Often codependency occurs in a family or a relationship where addiction or abuse is present. Bradshaw observes:

> Our society is highly addictive. We have 60 million sexual abuse victims. Possibly 75 million lives are seriously affected by alcoholism, with no telling how many more through other drugs. We have no idea of the actual impact on our economy resulting from the billions of tax-free dollars that come from the

illegal drug traders. Over 15 million families are violent. Some 60%
of women and 50% of men have eating disorders. We have no ac-
tual data on work addiction or sexual addictions. I saw a recent
quotation that cited 13 million gambling addicts. If toxic shame is
the fuel of addiction we have a massive problem of shame in our
society.[2]

What Bradshaw calls toxic shame, I define as soul loss. My experience reveals an alarmingly high incidence of soul stealing, especially in families and relationships where there is abuse and/or addiction. These dysfunctional systems can perpetuate the learned behaviors of codependency across generations. I believe that soul retrieval has many applications for counseling couples and families, but because the incidence of soul stealing is so high, we shamanic practitioners certainly have our work cut out for us in retrieving these stolen souls!

GOING TO THE LAND OF THE DEAD

In appendix A I discuss illness from a shamanic perspective; illness and even death may result from soul loss. Occasionally, the client's soul may have been stolen by malevolent spirits or even by the dead, who usually take it to the Land of the Dead. When this happens, the client appears to have died yet can be cured by the shaman, whose own soul enters the Land of the Dead at great risk to retrieve the client's soul. According to Åke Hultkrantz, shamanic stories include life-and-death battles between shamans and the inhabitants of that other world as they fight for the lost souls. Shamans retrieving souls from the Land of the Dead must be very strong and skillful.

In cases of disease through soul loss, the sick person is cured by a
medicine man of extraordinary ability, a shaman. The diagnosis

presupposes that the sick man's soul, generally the free soul, of its
own free will or by force has left the body. At times it may have
wandered off into the natural surroundings; at other times it may
have been carried away by malevolent spirits, especially the dead.
In such cases it is up to the shaman to send his own soul or less of-
ten, one of his guardian spirits, to retrieve the runaway soul. It may
happen that the soul which is carried away by the dead crosses the
boundary to the land of the dead, and when this occurs the sick
person dies. One who has "departed" under such circumstances,
that is to say, appears to the living to be dead, may be recalled to
life by a skillful shaman. Then the object for the shaman is to enter
the land of the dead, where he is in danger of being caught, and
bring back the soul in spite of opposition from the dead. Shamanic
tales from various places describe how the shamans battle for life
and death with the inhabitants of the other world, and how they
are pursued by the dead on the return journey.[3]

When I first began my work with shamanic journeying
eleven years ago I had a real fascination with the Land of the
Dead. My power animal refused to show me the way; he said I was
not ready. Another spirit helper tried to explain to me that there
were guards who stood at the entrance to the Land of the Dead
and that I had to learn to trick my way past them. The problem, I
was told, was that my heart was my vulnerable place. Because of
my "weak" heart I would be seen immediately and killed.

For the next two years I prepared to go to the Land of the
Dead. My spirit helper, a beautiful goddess of the woods, who always dressed in blue and had long gold hair, was to help me with
my heart. She has the same quality of being as the good witch of
the South from the books about the Wizard of Oz. For two years
she did healing work on my heart until my heart was finally replaced by a solid gold heart. For two years, three of my guardians
taught me how to walk with stealth in nonordinary reality, how

to make myself invisible, and how to fight if need be. Finally, after two years I was given a burgundy cloak to wear on my journey to the Land of the Dead. Now years later I have found all this preparation to be essential, because sometimes I have to go to this legendary territory to recover a lost soul.

Diana came to me for a soul retrieval. As an incest survivor, she carried the grief and anger of her experience with her but could not feel any resolution about her problem. Diana had been raped by one of her cousins in her teenage years. She now felt no sense of self, and the word *power* terrified her.

On entering the Lower World I find myself at a riverbank with a boat waiting there. Standing beside my boat is the guardian who accompanies me to the Land of the Dead; he is a skeleton. I put on my cloak and get into the boat, filled with an army of skeleton helpers that will row our boat through the dark murky waters to the island I am searching for. We row through the fog in absolute silence. I sit and try to quiet myself as much as I can, because for me to move through the Land of the Dead unharmed, I have to take on the appearance of one who has died. I need to hide my light and make my skin gray, to hang my head and depress all my life functions. As we row through a giant bone rib cage, I know we are getting very close.

The boat hits shore—the skeleton and his army will wait for me there. With my head hanging down and my body hunched over, I begin to shuffle toward the gate and past the guards into a landscape of death. There are high rock walls around me. All the rocks have scattered bones lying about on them. In the center of this place there are hundreds of other beings shuffling in a circle, all to themselves, all despondent, lost in absolute timelessness. There is no growth or hope, just silent pacing. I, too, pace along for quite some time, starting to feel exhaustion overtaking me. My life force has been depressed too long, and I am beginning to lose my will

Going to the Land of the Dead

to live. I know I have to move quickly or be lost myself. My power
animals can be of no help to me here. I am alone and have only
my own resources to draw on.

With my head still bent, I shift my vision as much as I can. The
only help I will get in identifying Diana among all these gray, life-
less faces is my intent. Now my attention is drawn to what seems
like an adolescent girl, who has the same dull look as the rest of

us. I shuffle toward her and start to pace beside her. "Are you Diana?" I say these words very slowly, and my words are slurred by my utter lack of strength. She nods. I take her hand, and I place my cloak around her. This cloak that was given to me allowed me to make us both invisible. We can slip through the gates unseen, as long as I can keep my light depressed. The only thing that can give me away is my light.

I pick up my pace a bit, pulling Diana, who has no ability to move any faster on her own, until we are safely beyond the gates of death. I collapse to my knees and breathe as deeply as I can, taking in life, feeding my cells with oxygen, visualizing my light. I thank the spirits for my life. I take Diana's hand, and we return to the waiting boat. The skeleton who never speaks nods at me, and we enter the boat for the long trip home.

As I step off the boat with Diana, I wave good-bye to my guardian and the army. We walk, as I practically drag Diana's soul to my place of power. There by the lagoon I sit looking at my reflection in the water. My power animal appears and sits next to me and Diana. He suddenly pushes me into the water, and the shock of the cold water wakes me up. I swim to a waterfall, where I let the water run over me and wash away my experience.

I swim back to where my power animal and Diana are sitting. My power animal gives Diana a potion to drink, and life begins to fill her up again.

My power animal explains to us that Diana's cousin was bitter and had been abused himself. He took out his anger and frustration and feeling of powerlessness on Diana, using rape and the idea of having power over her to deal with his own problems. He had taken Diana's soul and then discarded it in the Land of the Dead when he saw it did him no good.

I ask Diana if she is ready to return home. Diana thanks me for rescuing her from this place of no time, no life, no feeling.

Returning to ordinary reality seemed a little more difficult because I was very tired, but I was relieved to be home myself. From all that my guardians have ever taught me, I have learned that the Land of the Dead is not to be taken lightly. Diana and I ran up my tunnel back into ordinary reality and I blew her soul into her, lying patiently beside me.

When Diana sat up and opened her eyes she gave me a wide-eyed, very intense stare. The intensity of her gaze scared me a little, and I had to recenter myself. I asked Diana how she was doing. She took a very deep breath before she started to speak, and a shiver went through her body. She hesitated and continued just to stare at me. Finally she announced that she was okay but that she felt "weird." She began to shift her gaze away from me and to slowly look around my room. She wiggled her toes and rubbed her hands. I felt as if someone else were in the room with me.

I again asked her what she was experiencing right then. She said, "I feel so strong. I feel my body. I have physical sensations." One who has been numb for so long forgets what it feels like to feel. Diana spent a few minutes reorienting herself to being in her body before we discussed the journey. The strength she felt at this time was only a small sample of what she would experience later.

It took a few weeks for Diana to feel the power and strength of the adolescent who had left her. This adolescent now had a lot of life to catch up on. Diana found herself changing her diet. She felt she needed to eat "live food"—food that was green and fresh and had life to it. After changing her diet, she stopped smoking and drinking alcohol. And her spiritual pursuit was now directed toward a path of power and understanding the right use of power.

In soul stealing, a thief is dealing with the concept of power-over. This is not in harmony with the universe. To be in a universal flow, one must understand the concept of power *with* the forces of nature, not power *over* them. True power is transformative; it can transform any energy. With true power we can transform the negative energy of any illness. Ultimately with true power we can learn to transform all the illness that occurs on our earth, in our water, in our air. Ultimately with true power we can learn to transform suffering into joy.

Here is an exercise to help you remember your own light. Find a photo of yourself when you were a baby. Take a moment for yourself, and sit down with the photo. Close your eyes, and take a few deep breaths to center yourself. Open your eyes, and gaze into the eyes of the photo. See the light, and remember who you really are. That light is you, and unless you choose differently, no one can ever take that away from you.

PART III

WELCOME HOME: HEALING THROUGH WHOLENESS

The little girl comes to you

   cautiously   gingerly

does she dare

       to trust   again

She comes on dark wings

          with pink ribbons

wanting pretty things, ice cream

and a place

      in your heart

she whispers

      and wants you to listen

she is fragile and strong

        like a milkweed seed

   floating   looking for somewhere to land

if you nurture her, she will grow

     and bring you gifts

    of butterflies

—Ellen Jaffe Bitz

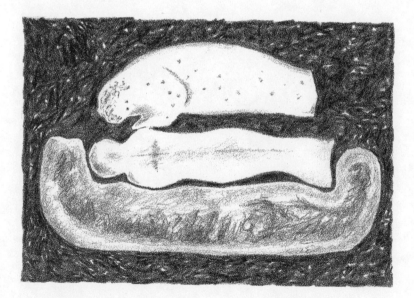

A Soul Returning

CHAPTER 8

EFFECTS OF SOUL RETRIEVAL

All sickness is homesickness.
—Dianne Connelly

The most difficult part of explaining soul retrievals to others is describing its effects. They vary so widely that there is absolutely no way to predict what will happen for a particular individual. We are each unique, and our psyche has its own way and timing for dealing with issues that come up. The effects of soul retrieval are extremely varied, both short- and long-term.

Soon after a soul retrieval people may report that they feel "more present" or "filled up." Some say they feel "bigger" or "lighter." Many discover that their senses are awakened, and colors are more vivid. They hear better, their sense of smell is awakened—they are more "in their bodies." People who came feeling ill and depleted often report feeling more energy, power, and strength immediately.

These changes can cause some disorientation for a few days, which is actually a positive reaction. When a person has been "out" of his or her body for thirty or forty years and is suddenly "in," everything seems a little different. It may compare to leaning to one side for years and then suddenly straightening up. One then experiences the world in a much different way.

I was very surprised at how disoriented I was after my own soul retrieval. Immediately after my session I had to drive Christina, who did the soul retrieval, sixty-five miles to the airport. I got into the driver's seat of my van, put my hands around the steering wheel, and stepped on the gas. I couldn't understand why my van wouldn't move. I picked up some shiny objects (my keys), staring at them and trying to figure out what to do with them. Needless to say, the ride to the airport was quite an adventure.

Let me suggest an exercise for you to try.

Look around the room you're in now, and find an object that attracts your attention. Go to that object, and sit in front of it. Close your eyes, and take a few deep breaths to center yourself. Now open your eyes, and fully focus all your attention on the object for just a couple of minutes. Look at every detail, study the color, notice the texture, concentrate, be aware. Now leave that object, and look around you. Bringing your awareness into the present to focus on the object might bring you fully into your body for a while. When you look around the room, notice whether from that state of heightened awareness you perceive things around you differently.

Sometimes a person becomes very giddy after a soul retrieval. Or a person may burst into tears, moved by the soul retrieval experience and the information. Tears often come if a memory of the trauma floods back in. We must remember that because the soul part left with the memory of the trauma, the memory returns with the part; the memory may come back immediately or over several weeks. Some people feel nothing immediately after the soul retrieval. Such a person might say, "I feel more peaceful," and leave, thanking me for my efforts and wishing me well.

I must admit that after I say the words, "Welcome home," I experience seconds that feel like minutes, filled with both anxiety and excitement as I wait for my clients to open their eyes and look into mine. What will happen? Sometimes the intensity of their gaze shocks and scares me. At other times the softness in their eyes makes me melt. Often the look is one of a mischievous child who has returned. This invokes my own mischievous child, and I just want to laugh. The wonderment of clients looking around with new senses always thrills me in doing this work. For some people it is like waking up from a very long sleep. For others it's like getting into bed at night, sinking down under the covers, wiggling around feeling the comfort and warmth, and sighing, "Aaaah!"

Sometimes the effect of a soul retrieval surprises a client, who might be geared up for an emotional backlash after getting back a certain soul part. When I worked with Jo, I brought back a part of her that left at age four when her mother would not allow the child to climb a backyard tree; little Jo was furious, and her strong-willed part left, angry at being told no.

The adult Jo was anxious about having her soul retrieval. She knew she had had a trying relationship with her mother but couldn't remember the details. When I reported the tree-climbing incident to Jo after I welcomed her home, she burst into laughter. What was such a big event to Jo at age four, an event that was terribly traumatic then, seemed so insignificant to a woman of forty who, by this time, had been told no many times.

The effect of the soul retrieval can often be surprising as the client reexperiences the event from an adult perspective rather than from a child's point of view. Frequently the incident does not seem as traumatic to the adult, although the child may have experienced it as shattering.

In most soul retrievals I find the effects are delayed about two weeks. Feelings of happiness, sadness, or anger seem to intensify over time. People might become temporarily depressed a few weeks after the soul retrieval; sometimes we must walk through the darkness to get to the light. Yet when clients have been chronically depressed, the return of the essence seems to spark the light of life they were looking for. Most people do, with time, feel the power, strength, and sensation of being present in their bodies. Many people notice that their dreams change significantly. Some people say their dreams become more vivid; many report that memories surrounding past trauma are shown in dreams. People who never remembered their dreams in the past begin doing so now.

A few people have told me that they experienced a preoccupation with death after a soul retrieval. Because soul retrieval marks an end of the "old" and a new beginning, this metaphorical death may be interpreted quite literally.

CHANGE

I am constantly amazed how these effects of soul retrieval change people's lives in a significant way. I have been inspired by the words coming back to me from people who have had soul retrievals, either with me or with other shamanic practitioners. Some of their accounts are included in the next few chapters. I thank each person for sharing these deep and intimate experiences so that we all can learn from them.

I also want to emphasize that in shamanism, we are working with the spiritual aspect of illness. From a shamanic perspective, emotional and/or physical illness is a lack of harmony in one's life. Although soul retrievals might correct what is out of harmony, this treatment sometimes needs to be complemented by other forms of therapy such as counseling, bodywork, or medical treatment.

GETTING MY SOUL BACK: PERSONAL EXPERIENCES

Earlier in the book I mentioned that the soul retrieval is not the end of the work but rather where the work begins. Clients spend an hour or two with a shamanic practitioner where the ceremony takes place. What, then, is the experience after they walk out the door and are finally alone with themselves?

Wendy describes her first soul retrieval, which brought back several parts.

When I got home I felt spacey and as though I were bringing home guests. I wished I had left my apartment neater; I was afraid the parts would not want to stay. I sat with great difficulty that first night and attempted to dialogue with my newly rejoined parts about what would help them to stay with me. The five-year-old almost jumped to the question and only requested that I add more fun. She liked the independence and freedom that I had in my life. As for the twenty-seven-year-old, I really couldn't get a clear answer to my question about what she needed to stay.

Over the next several days it became apparent to me that my day-to-day life had taken a turn. I became more focused and more organized and orderly, almost as if I suddenly had a manager or a force directing me. I feel that the twenty-seven-year-old needed to be needed, and she was answering my question with deeds. She saw that she could help and direct and have an active role in my life, and with that she would be happy.

Now even as I write this I realize that a third part was brought back from the deep underground, a very tortured, abused part. On that first evening when I asked what would help the parts to stay, the answer was a very soft, "Take care of me." In the weeks that followed I took care to be extra gentle with myself, almost as if caring for a child. I took longer baths, was more careful about meditation time, played softer music, used candles, and just tried not to add stress. I wanted the twenty-seven-year-old to know she was very loved, welcomed, respected, and protected.

Now almost six weeks have passed since my first soul retrieval, and the parts feel as though they integrated; I feel more present. I try to acknowledge the trauma each has suffered and thank them for coming back.

Sandee recalls the time following her soul retrieval:

Tuesday night, before falling to sleep, I asked my little girl to stay. I requested that in my dreams I should receive a sign or symbol explaining how to make a happy home for her. I had no recollection of a dream in the morning, but as the day progressed the image came to me of jumping rope with my mom and sisters. Before dinner, I did a relaxation meditation, then spoke to my little girl. Once again I asked her to stay. Was there anything I could do to keep her with me? "The only image that I've gotten was of jumping rope as a little girl. I will jump rope after this meditation, but what am I to learn?" Then as clear as a bell, a voice in my head said, "Learn to play."

I breathed deeply to relax again, then spoke to the second soul. I welcomed her home and asked what I could do to keep her with me. I quieted my mind, and several minutes later I was hearing the sounds of falling rain (a gentle spring rain, light but steady).

I called upon my third soul and, upon welcoming her home, asked what I could do to help her stay. I remained in a very relaxed state several minutes, and my mind was exceptionally clear. Then a tear flowed from beneath my eyelids down my cheek.

Soul Retrieval

I rose and went outside with rope in hand and jumped. Songs from my childhood were recalling themselves. Afterward, I sat down and enjoyed the warmth of the sunlight. With head in hand, I rested. When walking the dog before dinner, I felt a definite lightness about me, as if something had been lifted off my chest. Everything looked very clear, almost illuminated.

A PSYCHOTHERAPIST'S RESPONSE

Susann, a therapist in Denmark, sent me the following letter. After her own soul retrieval, she recommended it for several of her clients.

Dear Sandra,

Jonathan and I have now done about twenty to twenty-five soul retrievals, and I will try to write a few words about how a soul retrieval works for these clients with whom I have worked further.

In the year that I've worked together with Jonathan, I have become a more radical therapist, in that I work on freeing my clients from the bonds that tie them to their parents. (This is certainly the result of my own soul retrieval, which I will not go into here.) Many of the clients I have in therapy have grown up with parents who have rejected them emotionally, and it appears to me that in our culture, there is often a secret pact between parents and children that maintains that all parents do for their children is done from love.

I see a direct line from the point where this lie originates to the individual person's power center, which I call "the child." If children have always had to protect either their parents or themselves against their parents, all the power they should have used for their own development is lost and given instead to the parent(s).

The child's resources are used by others faster than the child can produce them. Such a child's loneliness is felt as a great sorrow. In some life situations, the lie cannot cover the fact, which has always been true, that the parent(s) have not been able to give love and protection to the child. These episodes lead to trauma.

It is these traumas I take my clients back to, and it is the chaos and emptiness surrounding these traumas that they are so afraid of feeling. For this work, the soul retrieval is a wonderfully effective tool for giving the power back to the child. With my previous therapeutic methods I have been able to teach my clients to mentally steer themselves away from situations where they become the victim. With soul retrievals I feel they get power back to the child, which they lost. I have noticed that several of my clients, after a soul retrieval, have reacted with anger, whereas before they felt guilt. Many of the people I work with are extremely exhausted and resigned after a long life of having produced energy only for the benefit of others. A soul retrieval gives them their energy back, in such a way that we can work together going through the traumas they have experienced, and a maturation is able to develop naturally.

Strong decisions are often made in the period after a soul retrieval. One woman, just before sending her daughter out into the world, is no longer afraid to see her as an independent individual. Another realizes that she has chosen the wrong career as nurse and would rather work in the business world. Still another woman suddenly remembers being sexually abused; a fourth becomes able to see how her mother had psychically terrorized her and starts to work with that issue.

I have one client with whom I don't think I've had a lot of success, because she continues to put herself into the victim role *in all life situations. Be that as it may, I would claim that after her soul retrieval she has become better at registering her feelings than she was before her soul retrieval. She had been sexually abused and had grown up in a fundamentalist religious environment, two factors I had often noticed previously among other clients.*

It has surprised me how many of my clients have declared their understanding of soul loss immediately, that they understand that they have lost some of their soul and that they need to get it back in order to be complete, powerful individuals. These concepts are logical to most of my clients, even though they have never investigated these nonordinary realms.

One therapist, Kevin, wrote to tell me about what his clients experienced with soul retrieval. He said that clients complained of being depressed, but instead what was really happening, he thought, was they were "not feeling" a lot before the soul retrieval. After a soul retrieval, however, clients find themselves experiencing more. Colors are brighter; the world is more textured, more sensual. People rediscover images that have a life of their own and find the magic of the child.

Kevin finds the difference in his clients' level of feeling to be immediate. Even negative feelings are experienced more fully. Clients have a sense of aliveness and a desire to live. In Kevin's experience, clients who weren't heavily traumatized feel better immediately after a soul retrieval, whereas those who have suffered more severe trauma seem to have more trouble after a soul retrieval. For these clients, follow-up counseling becomes crucial.

To have these soul parts back is both exciting and scary at the same time for most people. Will the connection be smooth? Will it be joyful? Will it bring pain? What demands will the returning soul make? Although these questions will be answered differently by each person receiving a soul back, the one thing everyone agrees on is that this is a great time of celebration.

LIMITATIONS OF THE WORK

Not everyone who comes for a soul retrieval experiences a dramatic effect—or even any effect at all. I'm a person who really enjoys the mysteries of the universe and doesn't believe that everything can be understood. Nevertheless, I see a variety of reasons why the effects of a soul retrieval may not be felt. First, the soul loss might not have been significant enough to produce seen or felt effects; the effect might be too subtle for the person to perceive.

Or some people may think they want a soul retrieval but on an unconscious level may not be ready to receive back their soul. They might not want to let go of their illness; the letting go of the old and familiar and the moving forward into the unknown just might be too threatening. Maybe they are not ready to handle consciously the return of memories. This need to wait must be respected. We are all unique, and our being's right timing for healing, change, and reexperiencing life traumas must be honored.

A person might think shamanism and soul retrieval are just "too weird." If the work is dismissed and invalidated, this could block any benefits.

Some people say to me, point-blank, that they don't want a soul retrieval. I sometimes hear this from incest survivors, who say, "I am not ready for my soul to come back." Again, I emphasize that I always honor this response and encourage people to seek help in preparing for the soul's return.

There are so many "roads to Rome"; shamanic soul retrieval is but one way to help someone attain a state of wholeness.

MORE TO TELL

There are many stories to tell. Each one is special and shows how soul retrieval can help us open ourselves to the power and beauty of the world around us, to be fully a part of that world.

Margaret, a dear friend of mine, writes:

Ever since I got my four-year-old back . . . oddly she is the most integral part of me. Joy as well as courage or just plain doing is at my disposal. It doesn't seem to be anchored or stayed . . . she seems to be the most fluid part of me. She is part of me and "is" whenever I want or need to feel her. But more than recovery . . . she is interdimensionally a window, almost a doorway that other dimensions can blow into or that I can go through to live or retrieve knowing from other dimensions. My memories flood over me, and integration is so comfortable, much more like a puzzle piece rather than a time bomb.

Larry writes:

One interesting effect seems to be that my perceptions and experiencing of what goes on around me seem to have more depth, a greater richness of "being." Things seem more "real," and I seem more part of them.

And Jessica, who suffered from chronic depression, sends some thoughts that flowed for her after soul retrieval:

Wanting to come home again, being one with self. Who can know where I have been but those who travel in the realms of darkness? Light rises to my eyes; it permeates my heart as I make peace with the creator—the creator of love, life, and magic. And who shall look upon my eyes and see but those who know, those who journeyed and saw the unseen territories where my soul has fled? To welcome myself home and create a home, a glorious

home where we are loved and happy and sit and bathe in the
light of life. Soul is a fountain of joy.

I received years ago in a journey this message: "The earth will support anything that supports life." What I have found after a soul retrieval is that one cannot "numb out" anymore. Each and every one of us must make personal and planetary decisions to stop abusing life. Whether a person has to give up an abusive addiction or eating disorder, change jobs, leave a relationship, take a more active political role, or increase awareness of how we continue to abuse our environment, we all now have to be responsible. Being responsible means responding to what is needed. We find a need to wake up and change our reality to a stance of "power with" Nature and the strength of being that knows all is possible.

CHAPTER 9

RELATIONSHIPS AND SEXUAL ISSUES

*The soul is the life whereby we are
joined into the body.*
—*Saint Augustine*

When we are fully home, a more realistic attitude about people around us seems to emerge. Some individuals feel it's easier to accept other people, maybe because now they can accept themselves. For others, a "reality check" might show that a relationship with a certain person is abusive and needs to end. Whatever the issue, many people find that the ways they relate to others do change. The following examples illustrate some different effects soul retrieval has on relationships.

Here is an excerpt from Antiga's journal:

It's the day after the soul retrieval workshop, and I'm beginning to realize how big a change I agreed to make when I asked for a certain part of my soul to be returned. When Sandy talked about how big the change might be, I felt scared. Was I ready? I decided that I could be scared and still go ahead, so I did.

The burning issue I had, and the piece that I asked Lynn, my shamanic practitioner, to bring back for me, was the part of my soul that accepts people as they are. Lynn's journey to find this part was interesting. She found her animals, went to the Lower

*World and Upper World and finally came back to me in the
Middle World and found it about a foot from my body. Lynn
and I agreed that the act of asking for the soul part had brought
it very close to me. I needed very little more to return.*

*Reflecting on what I need to do to keep this part of me, I real-
ized that speaking against others would need to stop. An understanding of what acceptance means came to me.*

*Acceptance is taking what I like and leaving the rest. "Leaving
the rest" includes not speaking about the part I'm leaving in a
put-down way (the part I'm leaving might be exactly what someone else needs). It includes understanding that putting down another person or system indicates that there is something missing
in my own self-esteem (soul). A much better use of my energy is
to find the missing part of me. Integration of this part can leave
me with no need to put another down. "Leaving the rest" does
not include being silent directly to a person whose behavior has
harmed me. Telling such a person how his or her behavior affected me is being respectful of myself. It enhances my self-esteem.*

*The part of this definition that asks me to change a lot is real-
izing that a system as well as a person may not be all bad. As a
feminist, I have spent twenty years of my life fighting the patriar-
chal system. Taking what I like from patriarchy and leaving the
rest (not speaking ill of it) is quite a challenge to me. Accepting
that there may be things I can use in this system and figuring out
what they are is part of the challenge. As with my decision to ask
for this part of my soul back, I am both scared and intrigued by
the challenge.*

Kate's soul retrieval prompted an assessment of her marriage:

In November of 1988 I was part of the soul retrieval workshop given by Sandra Ingerman. Saturday was the first day, and I had feelings of apprehension. As Sandra explained, to bring back part of the soul essence is powerful work and can sometimes ignite "forgotten" pain and often instigate life changes. The responsibility this carries was the root of my apprehension . . . the unknown wave that could rise within my life and the effect I could start in motion for another person as the retriever. Despite my fears I stayed in the workshop space. I felt an empty pit in my solar plexus, an emptiness that I have carried with me since early childhood. I hoped to find some nourishment, and to help others toward theirs. The aftermath of this weekend brought upheaval into my life . . . positive upheaval that put me, and is still putting me, into action.

When I was the client I had no idea what part of my soul, if any, the journeyer would be led to by his spirits. My mother had recently passed away, and our connection in life had been very complicated. In her passing it had still held this quality, and my mother often came to me in my dreams, once asking me to marry her. To be honest, there was a part of me that was afraid of her, as I always had been in life. I thought she might be hostile to the journeyer, as I felt sure she took a part of me with her upon her death. I let John, who was doing the soul retrieval for me, know this. He assured me that he trusted his spirits and would be protected. I relaxed somewhat. During the journey I stayed with my breath and remained in the room. When John finished and blew into my body, I felt a glimmer of what I will call fertility—just a glimmer . . . a drop. He recounted his experience and said he had met a baby of four to six months. This is the essence he returned to me. I thought, "OK, so what?" I did not know then the power of this infant.

The few weeks following this retrieval were very busy. I was closing on a house, working . . . on the run. Yet I was very energized despite my long hours. I also met three people who, on separate occasions, told me I looked different, that there was a fuller quality about me. At this time, I did not consciously associate these perceptions or my own fuller energy with the soul retrieval. I was too busy. By January of 1989, life slowed down as I moved into my new home and settled in. I had time to be with myself, and slowly feelings of depression began to creep in. I could not put my finger on the cause. I was finally living outside New York City with trees, stars, open space . . . all that I had been hungering for. Why should I be depressed? I kept on trying to put my sad feelings aside, but they began rising up stronger, until I spent days filled with crying. So much was pouring out of me, I thought my "rational side" would be swept away. I decided to seek professional help.

The person who was recommended to me by a friend held a master of divinity degree. I thought this was a good choice to help guide me through this upheaval of spirit. He did not quite understand my explanation of a soul retrieval, but was open, not judgmental. Having a person outside myself and outside my close relationships was a great help in sorting out my internal struggle. The realizations? I was in a weak marriage, a marriage that I had been accepting for years—accepting the emotional pain, the loneliness, the lack of sexuality—and this was taking away my strength. I am reclaiming my strength. I also realized that my way of functioning in this world was not healthy to myself. Big changes were in order. The crux is, the retrieval of a "lost" part of me made me more whole and therefore what was OK before in my life was no longer tolerable. This is growth. This gives me a stronger center from which to give back to this world.

I am less a member of the "walking wounded." (Author's note: Kate did leave her marriage after this realization and now has a much fuller life.)

Ursus writes about her soul retrieval:

Kerrith, my shamanic practitioner, told me of bringing back the following soul pieces: When I was about three years old, my father had taken away a doll I wanted very much. Kerrith found me sitting on the floor being terribly pathetic. She had her grandmother distract my father by cooking something in the kitchen and was able to get my doll back. When I was about eight years old, I was being knocked down by a big wave at the beach and thinking I would die. There was no one around to help me. (I do remember being knocked around by a wave and have in the past had recurrent dreams about tidal waves.)

When I was 18, I was in a car on the side of the road in a tropical setting. I have a knife in my hand. Kerrith asks me to come, and I say, "I'm all right," even though I'm not. She wants me to come, but I insist I want to stick the knife in the seat of the car. She finally convinces me to lay the knife on the seat instead, and I come along. (Three days before my eighteenth birthday I was picked up hitchhiking in the Florida Keys by a man who wanted to rape and kill me. There had been quite a few brutal killings there around that time—they found parts of women in many places—and I am convinced he was the killer. I managed to escape but was hurt pretty badly. I had a description of the guy and his car, but the authorities did nothing.)

When I was thirty: Kerrith specifically asked for this part. I was raped by a man who broke into my apartment. He stole part of my soul and forced me to take part of his. The part I had was well taken care of, shiny and full. The part he had taken from me was now tattered and torn, the life sucked out of it. Kerrith tricked him into taking his own back, because now it was obviously the more desirable one.

After my soul retrieval I felt much lighter and happier for the first time since I had been raped. My part said to go and find a stick and break it in half into the ground to represent the break between the man and myself.

My part was tattered and torn. When the police arrived [after the rape] they asked to take pictures of me as evidence. I had been through six hours of horror. I had the scarf around my head that he had used to blindfold me. I had mascara all over my face, which was bruised and swollen. Even though I never saw the pictures, I had one in my head. Part of my healing was to keep looking at this picture until I could feel compassion and love rather than fear, to embrace myself even in that moment I wanted to forget. (This had been true for all the parts.) It told me to buy a yellow scarf and wear it around my waist to remind me of the sunshine and happiness in life. A few days later I found myself singing that song, "Tie a yellow ribbon 'round the old oak tree; It's been three long years, do you still want me . . ."

The most remarkable difference, which began immediately after the soul retrieval, has been the lack of arguments between my husband and me. [Author's note: Ursus and her husband still have their problems to work out, but she reported the time following the soul retrieval as "the best time we have had together."]

During this time I felt lighter and happier. I had more confidence and more flexibility in my personality. I also had more

*vivid dreams—they seemed different, like on a different plane;
it's difficult to put my finger on it. I felt in tune with a deeper
level of myself.*

*The longer effects have been greater acceptance of my feelings
(I used to be upset about being angry all the time—now it's just
another feeling), much more control over my thoughts (I used to
be plagued with obsessive thoughts—now they are just gone),
and a greater sense of personal power. I also have noticed more
pleasant memories of childhood have surfaced. They might come
from a smell or being in a certain place—just nice little glimpses
of feelings.*

*Another truly wonderful thing has happened. I have become
more aware that each person is totally unique and has his or her
own unique gifts or viewpoints on life. I can only assume this is
happening because I am becoming aware that I am a unique
individual with my special talents and views. It's a very nice
perspective to have, and I am grateful to all those who have
made soul retrieval possible.*

As we move into right relationship with ourselves, it is so
much easier to move into right relationship with others. I also
find that we tend to pull people into our lives who mirror issues
that we are working on. For example, if I have a lot of unresolved
anger, I will pull a person into my life who expresses anger. If I
don't have confidence in myself, I might pull a person into my
life who is constantly putting me down. If I am fragmented, I will
pull in a person who is not whole.

When people welcome back their soul, their vitality, and
their original essence, light and the desire for true love and joy return. In maintaining this positive state, one seems to attract people
who have moved toward a greater sense of wholeness; they seem
to enter one's life to mirror and support the changes occurring.

I also find that a person who receives a soul back feels a responsibility to take care of the part that has been returned. For example, a person in an abusive relationship might take care of the retrieved soul part by leaving the relationship. In this type of situation the client's support system plays a crucial role.

In a dysfunctional relationship, there is an unconscious agreement between the two people (or the members of the family) to keep the dysfunction going. This is the role codependency plays. But what happens when someone in the relationship has an experience that causes that person to say, "I don't want to play this game anymore"? There is instant chaos; most likely, outside intervention will be needed. For the relationship to continue and grow, the other(s) must believe this change is good and must commit to working on themselves and the relationship. If this does not happen, the person who makes the change must decide whether to "numb out" and stay in a situation unsupportive to newly found wholeness or to leave the relationship. In one way or another, the balance will be upset, and some change will need to occur. A support system becomes essential either for counseling the relationship of the family or for helping the one who needs to divorce him- or herself from the situation.

Here's a dramatic case to illustrate the point. In the beginning of my work doing soul retrievals, I didn't yet have the big picture of its effects, so I didn't take the time in my interviews with clients to ask about their histories or support systems. Pam came to me asking for a soul retrieval. I did the soul retrieval, which was nothing out of the ordinary, and at the end of the session I wished Pam well. That night I received a phone call from a panicked Pam. She had been in a physically abusive marriage. When she got home she now felt whole enough to realize she couldn't stay there, but she had no place to go. At this point I had to refer her to an agency that could provide her with a safe place for her and her children.

RELATIONSHIP WITH FAMILY

After her soul retrieval Patrice had a hard time with family issues. I received a letter from her in which she described her experience:

> I think the biggest problem I'm having (and this is nothing new)
> is with my family. My inability to communicate with them (or
> their inability to communicate with me) on any level is probably
> the greatest source of pain and frustration in my life and has
> been, well, all my life. At this time, I don't want to have any-
> thing to do with my family. I have been struggling so hard with
> the issue that I'm OK and not a failure, a disappointment, or a
> bad daughter because I can't have a relationship with my family.
> But I get it from all sides: "Patrice is the crazy one in the family.
> Patrice has problems. Patrice is selfish and self-centered because
> she rarely calls or visits." I have intensely explored and worked
> on this issue for at least three years and still end up feeling infi-
> nite sadness and pain. I want a family. I really want only a few
> things in life, and a family is tops on my list, but that's not pos-
> sible for me, because I can't compromise myself any longer. I
> have to look out for my "children," my soul parts, and take care
> of them. They are—I am—my family. And I guess what I feel
> now is just a profound sense of loss. I know I'm not a selfish or
> coldhearted person, but the people I've wanted to be loved and
> accepted by forever think I am, and that hurts. And then I think,
> "How can I help other people through shamanism when I can't
> even deal with my family? What a fraud I am." Yet I can and
> have very effectively helped others, because I can be honest
> with them, be myself, and they appreciate that. I can't be honest
> and open with my family because I get nothing but derision, in-
> sulting and scathing judgment, and ridicule, sugarcoated with
> guilt and threats. Really, I'm not exaggerating. So the only way,

at this time, that I can keep myself healthy and happy and spiritually connected is to avoid my family. Are there others like me? Is it OK to have to do that? Or am I not being honest enough with myself about the situation? No, I am. I have been brutally honest with myself about how I contribute to this unfortunate demise of my family life, and I come up with the same answer every time: it's not me. It's not my fault.

So I'm now toying with the idea of changing my name, dropping my last name and using my middle name as my last name. Not only is [it] more pleasing to the ear, but it's a symbolic and tangible break with my family and my past. Well, I'm just pondering it.

I want to share this poem with you. Well, it's not really a poem because it doesn't rhyme, but . . . Even after the sorrow, the loss, the feelings of insanity, I know that my life is going to improve greatly because I'm more whole now, and because I refuse to give up. I do think the soul retrieval you did has marked a definite turning point in my life, and I'm very grateful. If you'd like to share this poem with others who want to know what can happen after a soul retrieval, go ahead.

I just had a soul retrieval today. Four pieces came back, and I've been smiling ever since. I've never felt so complete or so whole. I've never experienced such a solid sense of personal continuity . . . the gaps and chinks have been filled, the fissures erased. I embrace myself through the ages from three to twenty-one, from childhood to womanhood. How I admire who I am!

I say that without self-importance. I say it with true love and respect for the parts of me who returned today. . .for all they've been through, for their strength of survival, for their incredible courage to return to a life that had been all but

snuffed out. And those parts are truly me. The pieces of the
puzzle have been fit into place, and in time, the cracks will
disappear. I'll be one whole picture.

I look at the pieces now, each containing a vital part and
thus a painful memory, yet I feel joy. I review my life
and see such pain and misery, but I feel blessed. I have
lived a beautiful life. How can life be anything but beautiful
when you have soul? And now, I have soul.

My heart aches for those who have not got their souls back,
because only now, just today, do I realize the pain I was in,
the hopelessness I felt and believed was my future. But no
more. Today I turn to the path of Joy. Dear God in Heaven,
thank you for my life. There really is no place like home.

Deborah, by contrast, experienced a positive and healing
change in relationship with her family.

One of the most tangible effects of soul retrieval work I've done is
in the healing of my relationship with my mother. While jour-
neying at your workshop, I experienced myself as an infant at my
mother's breast. I experienced my enormous love and longing for
her, and I experienced what, as an infant, I interpreted as her re-
jection of me, as if I had done something wrong by my very pres-
ence, by even being born. This time on the journey, I took
another awareness with me, and I was able to know that what
I had interpreted as her rejection of me was really her own fear:
fear of poverty (by being pregnant, she had been forced to quit
her job, because that was the common practice in 1948); fear of
having the responsibility for an infant; fear that she would not
be able to take care of me. As an infant, I had interpreted her
anger as my having done something wrong by being born. This
time I knew that she was not angry at me, but at things that had
been done to her when she was a child, things she may never

name, may never remember consciously, but that have left their scars on her.

When I saw her about two months after the soul retrieval, I told her about my experience on the journey, and I saw her shudder. I saw the truth pass through her; I saw the fear on her face again. And, I saw a healing take place, her face soften when I, her forty-year-old daughter, named her experience.

She and I have acknowledged each other each time we've seen each other during the last year. In March, during the time of my grandmother's birthday celebration, we sat at the dining room table with extended family. I asked my mother about the places we had lived when I was a child. I said I remembered the apartment where we lived when I was an infant but couldn't remember the one where we lived when I was a toddler. My great-aunt "tsked" and said I couldn't possibly remember something from my infancy. My mother said, "Oh, Deborah remembers." A healing passed through me; the infant in me felt affirmed.

During this last visit, we even talked about the way she treated me when I was a child. "I know you think I abused you," she said to me in the midst of tears. I dropped my eyes and reached into my heart for the words that forgive, for the words that would not accuse and wound and keep us apart, but that would heal both of us. "I know that you did the best you could. I know that the way you treated us was not a fraction of the abuse you had experienced when you were a child, and that in the 1950s some people believed that you had to paddle children to force them to obey. And I have carried the wounds of that treatment with me all my life. I know that you thought you were doing right, and I have had to do a lot of work to untie the knots that got twisted inside me. I do not blame you. This is not about blame. We can only forgive ourselves and each other, and move on."

*More healing. More parts of me returned. More parts of me
staying home. I do not need to abandon myself in order to forgive
my mother.*

The marital relationship often improves after soul retrieval.
Donna, like many others, reported she stopped being so angry at
her husband, realizing that her own life's frustration was being
displaced onto him. She now had what she needed to create her
own happiness. I get a lot of feedback that spouses stop arguing
with each other after one has had a soul retrieval, because that
person becomes more independent and capable of making life-
giving choices. Sometimes one spouse will encourage the other to
come for a soul retrieval to enhance the opportunity to grow together.

You can see how soul retrieval can create both positive and
problematic effects. It can help to relieve the stress between people in a relationship; or it can cause more stress if the change in
behavior alters the dynamics of a relationship or family in which
the other members are unwilling to change as well.

INCEST AND ABUSE

Chances are that one-third of the women and one-fifth of
the men coming to me for a soul retrieval are survivors of incest or
sexual abuse. This is a significant proportion of the population.

Any kind of abuse—sexual, physical, or emotional—will
cause soul loss. The child feels invaded and powerless. Innocence
is gone, and life no longer holds the grace that comes from innocence. The world suddenly becomes a very unsafe place to be.

The complex issue of abuse has been quite frustrating for
people to deal with. For all survivors there is a range of complicated emotions related to their past, including guilt, shame, invalida-
tion, love, hate, and humiliation, among others. Varying with the
age and the extent of trauma, the effects can include dissociation

or fragmentation, depression, eating disorders, illness, or abusiveness toward others. The fragmentation and dissociation can even be so severe as to result in multiple personality syndrome. The healing journey for survivors can be long and arduous, filled with dark spaces and many pitfalls.

If, like the old tribal societies, we had a stronger sense of community, would sexual and/or physical abuse of children be tolerated? Probably not. These behaviors would have been controlled purely by peer pressure. But because this is not the case, a large part of our population is among the "walking wounded."

For psychotherapists it is not a new concept that people who have experienced abuse "leave" their bodies to survive the ordeal. Traditional systems can work well with this condition. But as a shamanic practitioner working with sexual abuse and soul loss, I see how the essence splits off from the survivor and actually leaves the body to go to nonordinary reality. These souls are often frightened, confused, sad, and/or angry, and they need to come back. As long as they are floating in nonordinary reality, the adult is not free to move forward. The vision and psychic energy aren't there to create a self-nurturing life. Once the missing part returns, the client can finally progress in therapy toward creating a healthier life.

A CASE STUDY ON SEXUAL ABUSE

Karen was a thirty-eight-year-old woman who in the last five years had started to remember incidents of sexual abuse as a child. She was in psychotherapy and found this to be a great help not only in dealing with the memories that were surfacing but also in coping with daily life. Her therapy was falling short, however, in helping her reclaim her "child."

Karen felt that her life was shattering around her. Her marriage was disintegrating. Her husband was an alcoholic and couldn't give Karen the emotional support she needed at this point in her life. She had little understanding of how to set boundaries between herself and other people—how to know what were her feelings, needs, and desires rather than those of her husband, friends, and family. Karen was overweight. When she ate food, she had no sense of what it was like to feel full; she complained of an empty hole inside her that felt very dark and endless.

Karen was working on all these issues in therapy. She wanted to tell me her story before we began her work. It is not necessary for me to have this information to do a soul retrieval, but Karen felt it was important for me to know what she was dealing with. Hearing Karen's story before I began my work created a heart connection between us, which always makes my intention seem more profound.

My biggest concern in working with Karen was knowing there was a good possibility the effects of soul retrieval would upset the dynamics she had at home. She seemed so fragile. We talked for quite some time about her support system and her commitment to therapy. I brought up the issue of change and the temporary disruption that change can sometimes cause. Without preprogramming Karen about what changes to expect but instead talking about the concept of change in general, I questioned her about whether she felt it was the right time for a change in her life-style to occur. She said she was working on this in therapy but that she had never been asked this question so directly. I encouraged her to honor herself and spoke about right timing. I'm never one to try to "push the river."

I could see Karen's mind trying to kick in and interfere with her going to a deeper place inside herself. She said my observation was true. She was hearing the "tapes" of old messages from her mother, her husband, and other authority figures telling her what and what not to do.

I led her in a guided meditation (see the exercise at the beginning of chapter 1), teaching her how to discern intuition coming from a deeper place from "mind chatter." It took a while for her to find her bodily cues for truth, but she did get them. She felt a warm feeling in her body when she was experiencing a deep truth, in contrast to feeling a tightening of her heart and that she couldn't breathe when she was telling herself a lie.

We jointly decided that it would be best for Karen to use her body cues in deciding whether she was ready for a soul retrieval. She did request a power animal retrieval at this time. This would be a safe way to go, because the power animal would be able to give Karen the strength and energy she needed to deal with her choices. It would also give her an experience of working with me and of the sensation of my blowing power into her body. Having someone blow your soul into your body can make you feel very vulnerable. Blowing a power animal into the body is not as intimate, and it helps a person become comfortable with the method. I wanted to be sure Karen was working in partnership with me and didn't see me as another perpetrator.

> When I get to the Lower World, I meet my power animal and tell him I am looking for an old power animal who was once with Karen to come back and help her at this crucial time in her life. I enter a canoe that I always use with my power animal when we are looking for a lost power animal. We descend into a long, winding river bordered by thick Amazon jungle. The sun is shining very brightly, and the air is thick with moisture. My clothes are beginning to stick to my skin as I paddle, watching the banks of the river carefully for the appearance of animals.
>
> I hear the chattering of birds in the trees, and I am aware of animals drawing close to the shore, curiously watching our journey down the river. The journey is smooth, as the water is quite calm

*with no rapids in sight. This makes me very happy, because I get
seasick easily.*

*A giraffe appears on the shore, running after the canoe. The
giraffe is obviously not there out of curiosity; she is making very
clear eye contact with me. But I must see the giraffe or some
aspect of it four separate times before I will bring it back to Karen.
The appearance of the giraffe four times signifies it agrees to
return to Karen. I then see an eagle in the sky screeching at me.
After that a group of elephants begins to march through the trees.
I paddle calmly and watch. Out of the corner of my left eye, I see
another giraffe on the left bank. And then another giraffe joins the
second giraffe. Finally, a fourth giraffe makes a huge leap from
the right bank and lands in the canoe, shaking it dangerously for
a few minutes. This is an obvious sign of the giraffe's intention
and commitment. I don't waste any time, and we paddle back up
the river very quickly. Our boat lands, and the giraffe and I together return back to ordinary reality via my tunnel. Clutching her to
my heart, I blow the giraffe into Karen.*

Karen felt a great deal of heat going through her body. I told
her that heat is a sign of power. When I told her a giraffe came
back to offer power to her, she giggled at the prospect of having a
giraffe as a power animal but liked the idea a lot. Because the giraffe agreed to come back to help Karen, there was nothing Karen
needed to do except welcome it and know the giraffe was there to
protect her and give her strength.

At this point we decided to end our session. Two hours had
gone by in ordinary reality. I told Karen that she could call me if
she wanted to go further with our work together.

Two weeks later I received a call from Karen saying she was
ready for a soul retrieval. When Karen returned, I asked her if she
could say to me clearly and from a place of truth that she was
ready for her soul to come back. She looked at me intently and

answered, yes. She also said that she had told her therapist about what she would be doing and that her therapist was ready to help with anything that might arise from our work together.

I called in the helping spirits and gathered my power to me by singing my song. When I no longer had a sense of being present in the room, I lay down next to Karen.

> *My entry into nonordinary reality is quick. I am moving very fast into the Upper World. I come to a blinding light and see Karen as a three-year-old child standing in the light. It seems that she is actually holding hands with the light. She is strong. She has quite a powerful presence, and I see clearly from her stance and the penetrating look in her brown eyes that she has a very strong will. I introduce myself to her. "Karen, my name is Sandy, and I'm a friend who would like to bring you home."*

> *She says, "I know who you are." She is a tough little girl!*

> *I laugh at her bullying voice. "You know, Karen could really use your help down there. She's forgotten how to play, and she misses the power, strength, and will you left with. She feels so empty without you."*

> *Karen says, "Okay, I'll come back, but things are going to have to be different or I'll leave again. You know I know how to leave again."*

> *"I know you do, Karen," I reply, "and thanks for trying."*

> *Then she says, "But we can't go back until we find the thirteen-year-old."*

> *"Do you know where she is?" I ask.*

> *Karen takes my hand and pulls me from the light down into the Middle World without any hesitation. I really like this child and admire her power. We come to a soul that looks like Karen at thirteen. She's just floating aimlessly through the stars, following the earth in a circular direction. She has a confused look on her face.*

"Karen," I call to her. She continues to float aimlessly, not responding to my voice at all. Three-year-old Karen takes her hand and pulls her to an abrupt stop. I like this child. I want to follow her around for a while; I think she has a lot to teach me.

Then the little Karen tells me the thirteen-year-old's story. "When Karen got her period and her body changed, she got real confused. She was afraid of what would happen to her now." I understand the dilemma. I see it so often with women, especially those who have been sexually abused. The fear of being a sexual woman is quite overwhelming, and a person's not wanting to own this phase of life so often causes soul loss. I face the thirteen-year-old and explain to her that she has a lot of wonderful gifts in store for her coming into womanhood and that there are people back home who will help her with this. The three-year-old looks at her with a twinkle in her eyes and says, "Will you come home with me?" The thirteen-year-old Karen agrees, and we fly through the sky with warp speed. I clutch both parts to my heart and blow them back into Karen.

After welcoming Karen home, I told her about the three-year-old and the thirteen-year-old. I described the strength, power, and strong will I experienced from her, and she began to laugh and cry simultaneously. She said, "I know that little girl." She thanked me for bringing her back. She could also relate well to the story of the older child and made a strong commitment to herself, with me as fair witness, that she would work on her issue of being fully a woman.

With the strong will of the three-year-old spurring her on to work hard, Karen made great progress. Her little-child part taught her how and when to say yes and no to others in her life. Over time she began to get a better sense of who she was as separate from the rest of the world. At first this difference in Karen caused disruption in her marriage as the dynamics of the relationship changed. But then Karen's husband went into therapy himself to work on his own power issues. They eventually went into couple counseling. Karen hopes that one day he will be open to seeking soul retrieval, but she respects his own timing with this.

As Karen embraced the three-year-old and the thirteen-year-old inside her, her life took on a different meaning. She felt a strong desire to create a nurturing life for her lost children. They met a need in her that food had filled, and she found herself losing weight naturally.

As Karen lost the weight, the issue of her being an attractive woman became a focus for her therapy. She also decided to receive bodywork to help release the old memories in her body and wake up her awareness of being "in" her body. At first this shift was quite scary for her. She had cut herself off from her bodily sensations for so long that the new energy felt a bit too raw and overwhelming. But she had the support of her giraffe, her three-year-old, her thirteen-year-old, her therapist, her husband, and me, cheering her on. Karen was excited about the possibilities before her and had a very strong will to experience life fully with the new understanding she gained from her hard work.

Patrice, who has been suffering with fibromyalgia, tells her story:

> I've begun having clear memories . . . more than memories, they're so clear it's as if I am actually there. But they are good memories. The good ones are coming back first, thank God. What I relived yesterday really touched me. It lasted about an hour . . . it was
> the time I was a camp counselor at a music camp when I was twenty-one. At this time, my illness was just starting, in the very early stages; I was just noticing that I wasn't feeling very well. I realized as I walked (I relived this on my morning walk) that

one too many soul parts had left, too much of my essence was gone, and what was holding on to life, to the hope of a decent life, was my body.

Fibromyalgia is a nasty muscular disease caused by an underlying sleep disorder and is characterized by chronic tightness and soreness of the muscles, just the way one would be if one were holding on to something too tightly, too long. So on my walk I realized this, and physically felt the way I did at that age, which was 150 percent better than I do now. It was nice to have that glimpse of relative health. And I really understand illness now in terms of soul loss. My physical state was not caused so much by what I had as by what I didn't have . . . my essence. I still have a lot of work to do on this issue, but I am working hard. I've decided to try to write some articles on this issue, particularly from the perspective of fibromyalgia and sexual assault. I've read tons about this disorder, but no one has made any connection between the two, which amazes me. Ninety percent of people with this disorder are women; one out of three women has been molested. I also had a touching realization Monday night when I went to bed. I talked to my parts and tucked them into bed (boy, have I been a busy mom lately). As I spoke to my five-year-old, I spontaneously whispered the phrase, "It's safe to sleep now." It was then I realized that perhaps that's why I've been unable to get deep sleep for years—it wasn't safe. And then I remembered being afraid to sleep as a child because I didn't know who might be coming into my room. Anyway, lots of memories and realizations these past few days.

After Suzanne had her soul retrieval, she wrote me, saying:

Since my soul retrieval, I have made the conscious decision to stay on this earthly plane. The fact that we are spirit has mean-

ing to me. I am slowly transforming that spirit into material.
Because I was able to make the conscious decision to be alive,
I feel I am getting a second chance that few people have. I have
been reborn—with me and God as parents. Right now I feel as
vulnerable, excited, and scared as a newborn baby, but this time
I have forty-some years behind me to give me strength and
knowledge.

A few months ago I received a phone call from a woman who had a soul retrieval with one of my students. She is an incest survivor who had spent years in therapy trying to no avail to recall the memories of her experience. She said she could not remember, could not recall details of the experience, including the act itself. She wanted to let me know that after the soul retrieval, the memories finally came back in a very gentle way so that she had the strength to deal with them. I find this often to be the case, for really the universe is out to help and heal us, rather than being out to "get" us.

Little girl, small child   where are you

Brown legs, hard feet, hands never large enough

Yellow hair with a will of its own

Brown eyes that could not see

And a mind that could take you away

Where did you go

You took some things that I need now

You have hidden yourself well

I have been trying for so long now to make

  a way for you to come back

I think that it is safe now

And I want to know you.

                    —Anonymous

CHAPTER 10

LIFE AFTER SOUL RETRIEVAL

If you really want to help this world,
what you really will have to teach
is how to live in it.
—Joseph Campbell, in an interview
with Bill Moyers

The human body, left up to itself, is in a continuous state of death and rebirth, shedding and regrowing. Our old skin constantly sheds, and new skin grows. Our bones constantly shed old fractures, and the bone regenerates. Our blood takes away toxins so organs can eliminate them from the body, and new blood circulates, feeding our organs. When there is a breakdown in this process, illness occurs. We have an ego and psyche that are part of our inherent being. Our psyche constantly works and changes through our dream state. The ego, whose true function is to perceive time and space for us, has become very complex and doesn't always follow the flow of life. Life is change, but many of us find that the ego holds on to pain, fear, anger, and hurt when it could let them go and continue to flow, grow, and evolve as all of our other systems do.

Whenever energy gets "stuck," it creates illness. If the soul has fled and the ego is stuck at the traumatic time, the being is no longer in harmony, and there is illness. Whether physical, or emotional, or spiritual illness, the being will manifest some problem at being stuck. Depression results when energy stops moving. How many times have you been able to change a problematic state of consciousness by physically moving your body—whether by exercising, hiking, or jogging—so your energy starts flowing again?

Once you bring the soul back, it is time for the ego and the body to let go of the stuck place and help us move and evolve to be once again in harmony with all of life. In this chapter I will discuss life after soul retrieval. How can we use shamanism, ritual, psychotherapy, and bodywork to help a person release pain, which is just part of nature, to shed and grow and take his or her rightful place on the earth? How can our newly regained soul parts act as allies for us in creating a whole life? We cannot move into an adult way of being if we are stuck back in childhood. We need to live fully in the present.

Soul retrieval is not a form of therapy that keeps us stuck in our past; it is a step in closing the doors on the places in life that have blocked our own growth and evolution. Furthermore, I have no intention of teaching a method that unleashes adults acting like children out in the world. The key here is partnership. How do we get body, mind, spirit, and all our soul parts working together for a common goal—living to our highest potential? I cannot stress enough the importance of continuing to work with the parts that have returned. These parts have been gone for years, and when they return, they must be listened to. They come back as allies, bringing a wealth of information.

IMAGINATION AND VISION

A few years ago I was journeying just to check in and "hang out" with my power animal. I don't want to abuse the relationship I have with him by seeing him only when I'm asking for information. We were sitting together in my power place in the Lower World, having a picnic. Suddenly he began to talk to me about Walt Disney. He told me that Walt Disney's work on earth had been to stretch people's minds and imaginations. One must stretch the imagination, for example, in order to embrace the image of a walking, singing guitar. To the logical mind, this image does not make any sense. Walt Disney was trying to teach people to imagine.

How can we envision a healthy body or mind or planet if we cannot imagine it? Because of today's technology—television programs and movies, which don't leave much to the imagination—we have let our ability to imagine become dormant. I think the population that best shows us the extreme of what happens when we lose the ability to imagine and envision is teenagers today. We are actually seeing a group that have lost their souls, and one major reason is that they can't envision either their personal futures or a bright future for the planet.

Bringing back the child in a soul retrieval restores our ability to imagine. Then we can begin to use creative visualization to manifest our dreams as well as our health. But we must find a way to keep the lines of communication open with these retrieved parts.

THE SOUL RETURNS WITH GIFTS AND KNOWLEDGE

A soul part that returns might have the knowledge the person needs—for example, how to trust, love, write, create, play, or be self-confident. How can the client make contact with the part so as to work in connection with it? If a part comes back that left because it was abandoned, how does one give it enough love to stay so that one can remain whole again?

The way I work with this in my own life and practice is to

journey to these parts. I actually have a client's power animal or teacher set up a meeting in nonordinary reality with the returned soul parts. Here they can dialogue with each other, discovering what changes are needed for integration.

Many of us have already seen how some form of counseling can be effective in creating change in our lives, maybe through personal experience or by watching a friend or family member go through the process. My experience shows that the work goes much faster and deeper by adding the spiritual component of soul retrieval. We have already seen in a number of the case studies and letters how people were able to resolve some deep issues and release behavior patterns that were following them. Remember the Danish therapist who reported that after soul retrieval, most of her clients stopped playing the role of "victim."

GROWING UP

One of the differences between the adult state of being and the child state of being is that a child is dependent on adults for security and physical survival. As we become adults, we acquire the ability to create our own reality. To some extent children can do this as well, but ultimately they are growing, establishing an individual identity, and learning about the nature of reality in a different way than adults do. From the information gathered throughout their lives, with imagination and belief, adults have the opportunity to make choices that bring them closer to realizing their dreams. But this also takes a willingness to be responsible and powerful. I find in teaching and working with people that power has become a great "hot potato." Who can I throw it to, so I don't have to hold onto it? Who can I give my power to? Who can I give responsibility for my life, my behavior, my problems? Every time we relinquish our power, we release our energy; we give away a piece of our soul.

CHOOSING LIFE

In the beginning of this book I wrote about my own journey from the darkness. Earth was not home for me, and for years I craved to leave life here. My own soul retrieval was such a miracle! I had no expectations about what would happen. I was just trying to teach Christina the method and used myself as a person to practice on. Getting my soul back instantly snapped me out of a depression that had lasted for more than twenty years. I don't know why my soul left; I just know my little girl came back. When I go inside myself, I see her giggling all the time. She's even come out to write a portion of this book (you can probably see what parts she did write).

But from a place of wholeness I learned that the teaching "we experience what we believe" is really true. In a lecture I once heard, a spiritual teacher said, "Most people think we believe our experience. This is not true; we experience what we believe." Think about that for a moment; it is a bit of a mind twister.

I believed that life was just too hard, and whenever things went well the universe would find some way to pull the rug out from under me. After my soul retrieval, however, life became much easier. I could see the beauty around me, and I realized, with the lessons from the spirits, that life on earth is really a gift. That's why so many spirits take on human form. Spirits don't get to touch or smell or really experience the sensation of being alive. Through the patient nudging of my spirit helpers, I made the commitment to be here fully and to take total responsibility for my life. What I found, to my surprise, is that everything became simpler. I found the universe was not "out to get me" but was there to give me what I was asking for. My fragmentation not only caused my depression, but it diluted my commitment to being here. Because my commitment wasn't strong, the universe reflected that back by not always presenting me with life-giving situations. Because I was fragmented, I couldn't hear or see well in this reality. I was rarely aware of my environment, because I was out of my body half the time. I wasn't listening fully, and I missed a lot of signals that could have helped me avoid making some disastrous decisions.

With the help of my spirit helpers, this has all changed. I'm not saying I don't have bad days—I do. But I also have the tools to change those bad days if I again take a stance of power, power being the ability to transform any energy. Life has become a lot more meaningful and fun. I've also learned how as an adult I can work in partnership with the spirits to create my visions, instead of expecting them, as a child would, to create my life for me.

USING RITUAL FOR INTEGRATION AND HEALING

Ritual is another very powerful way to help people release problems or patterns that no longer serve them. The nature of ritual is that it creates change. Ruthie, for example, was given a ritual that her shamanic practitioner obtained in the same journey in which she did the soul retrieval. Through this ritual Ruthie could both retrieve a part of herself that her father had and get him out of her heart as well. Her ritual involved breath work. For one minute in the morning and the evening, over a ten-day period, she was to bring her heart "in" while inhaling and send his part back to him on exhaling. She was to envision this and work with her breath. After ten days she was to send him something with a heart in it and give herself something with a heart in it. Ruthie baked her dad his favorite cookies and sent them to him in a heart-shaped box. She bought herself a clay Christmas ornament with two doves on it. She still uses the ornament every year on her Christmas tree. Ruthie's therapist gave her the crystal soul catcher used in her soul retrieval. Ruthie uses this crystal during her visualization work and reports that the crystal still holds special meaning for her.

Her therapist says that Ruthie has slowly been able to be more and more herself. She had a paranoid quality and a sense that she would "disappear," which her therapist thought was connected to her soul having been stolen. After completing her ritual, Ruthie is "settled" and comfortable with herself now.

Bonnie was also given some homework to do after her soul retrieval. Her ritual was very elaborate. Here is the letter I received from her:

> During the soul retrieval itself, I remember having to pretty continuously remind myself not to "leave the room." The room we were in has a skylight, and it is easy for me to dissociate by staring into that lighter place and then going into it. I also remember three sensations, perhaps like sensing an inner "bump" or jolt, during the soul retrieval.
>
> Immediately afterward I experienced a feeling of melancholy that lasted for several days. A sense of not wanting to be "jostled" lasted for perhaps a month or more. I felt fragile, and I did not want the newly integrated parts to break off once again. I was afraid that if that happened, they would not ever want to come back again.
>
> I was told to meditate every day for eight days on anger and hatred, put it in something symbolic that would burn, and burn it. Immediately after meditating I was to rub down with oil scented with lemon. I chose to put the anger in a bowl of wadded-up paper and sage.
>
> The first night, the evening of the soul retrieval, I meditated by letting white light flow into my body through my heart and

shoulders. As the light circulated through my body, a black, thick substance began to flow out of my hand onto the paper and sage. Gradually the blackness inside became smoky and continued to flow out until I was all white inside. The three retrieved parts of my soul and I sat together, and I talked to each one, verbalizing my commitment not to hurt them. I showed them my house, and they liked it.

I then got up, went out [onto] the front porch and burned the paper and sage in the bowl, avoiding inhaling the smoke. After the fire went completely out, I scattered the ashes in the yard. Finally, I went inside and rubbed myself down with massage oil and lemon, covering all of my body as if to create a boundary.

Each of the eight nights I followed the same ritual, and each of the nights I noticed a progressive change.

By doing her burning of paper and sage each night and working with the fire, Bonnie watched her anger dissipate. She started to realize how she kept her anger alive by feeding it, just as one feeds a fire. She also realized as she waited each evening for the embers to die out that she should not expect a sudden change in her anger, that she needed patience. Bonnie continues:

On the eighth night I again saw green shoots poking through the ash, and they appeared to have grown and spread. When I went out to burn the paper and sage, the burning proceeded as usual. Then, as the embers began to fade, a wind came up, scattering the dying ashes out of the bowl, around the porch, and across the front yard. The wind appeared to come from several different directions. I realized that change, too, comes from any direction and carries one in unforeseen directions. It just takes being ready, and willingness. This is letting go.

*I should mention that each time I meditated I connected
with the three retrieved parts or selves, and talked with or held
them. I felt a little awkward, but it conveyed caring, which I
very much wanted them to know about. I apologized to them
for my neglect of them and anger at them and for what
they had been through. The three-month-old would look back
at me and maintain eye contact. The older two became less
angry, by degrees. Even the fifteen-year-old relaxed sometimes.*

*About eight months later, I met with a nutritionist-healer who
told me that if I had not done the soul retrieval, I would have
become sicker. She also told me that in Native American tradition, when a ceremony is complete, a wind comes up, signifying
the end.*

MANY FORMS OF HEALING

The ego is not the only part of us that needs to shed the
past so we can move forward. Many of us hold past traumas in
our bodies. One can even look at oneself in the mirror and see
where energy is blocked and not moving. I've found that another method of integrating the soul is to have bodywork done.
There are so many bodywork systems that I won't try to name
them all here. A person might choose gentle massage, for example, or a bodywork therapy that requires more muscle manipula-
tion, or acupuncture, which gets the *chi* flowing (*chi* means "life
force").

If we are truly moving toward integrating body, mind, and
spirit, we must pay attention to all these areas. For severe illness,
we can also turn to Western medicine, remembering not to give
our power away to doctors but to work in partnership with them.

We must recognize that our bodies might need medical treatment to help to release disease from the body.

In traditional cultures shamans and other healers worked together; they were not in competition. What might heal one person might not heal another. Because our knowledge of human beings has become so complex, the new challenge has become seeing what system—or systems working together—succeeds for each person. We cannot just choose one or enter into some form of healing by just going through the motions. I truly believe that if the commitment and the willingness to take some responsibility for our healing are strong, healing will come.

AVOIDING FURTHER SOUL LOSS

There are still two questions about life after soul retrieval that need to be answered. The first involves how to avoid further soul loss. Sometimes soul loss is necessary. If one is in a car accident or suffers some other physical trauma, for instance, the loss of the soul helps one survive the experience. If people were to remain totally present during such traumas, I don't know whether they could stand the pain and survive.

But in other situations we do have some control. If the presence of another person makes you feel drained, as if your energy is being "sucked out of you," then protect yourself. Call power to you. Surround yourself with light, or visualize yourself in a blue egg to create a boundary between you and the other person. In relationships and in your life, work on becoming an adult. Whenever possible, avoid giving away your power or energy to others. Create a community around you by finding friends who have a deep commitment to living in a positive way. And just try to remember that giving a piece of yourself to someone else doesn't serve you or the other person or the situation.

HOW MANY SOUL RETRIEVALS DO WE NEED?

A second question that comes up concerns the number of soul retrievals that are needed. I don't think people need a lot of soul retrievals. In classical traditions a soul retrieval was given only after a trauma had occurred, if a serious illness manifested, or if a person was in a coma. Sometimes I have to work more than once. This is true even in tribal societies, where the shaman sometimes had to work three days in a row on behalf of the patient.

I've had a rather bizarre vision of soul retrieval clinics set up around the country, where after a hard day at the office, or after a fight with someone close to you, or just a bad day in general, you could go stand in line and get your soul retrieved. But in all seriousness, I believe that once you have enough significant parts of yourself, maybe the rest will follow. I find that most people don't require many soul retrievals. After one or two, most people have back what they need to experience wholeness in their lives. Depending on a person's condition—a serious physical illness, a psychotic state, or the aftereffects of an extreme trauma—the course of treatment might need to involve more work.

DOES EVERYONE NEED A SOUL RETRIEVAL?

I believe that we all have suffered some soul loss during the course of our lives. But that doesn't necessarily mean we all need a soul retrieval. The questions that need to be addressed are these: Do you feel there is a significant problem with how your life is functioning? Do you struggle with the symptoms outlined in chapter 1? I encourage people to seek out healing if there is a problem. We can all work on creating a better life for ourselves, but a specific healing technique such as soul retrieval isn't always necessary for change to take place.

Life after soul retrieval is about learning how to live in this world. Now that we're here, now that we're home, how do we move around in our home, redecorate it, rebuild it into a beautiful and comfortable place to be? And how do we update our whole being—body, mind, and spirit—to live fully in the present?

Here's a ritual you might want to try on your own. What you need for it is a small offering to the spirits. I see an offering as a gift from the heart, so if you have some small object that you would like to leave on the land, that would be fine. The native people in this country often leave cornmeal or tobacco without chemicals in it as a gift. The outward value of the gift makes no difference.

Once you have your offering, go out to a place in nature. It can be your own backyard or a park. Take a few deep breaths, and center yourself. Now reach your hands high into the air, and imagine yourself fully embracing the sun with your arms. Close your eyes, breathe deeply, and experience yourself as fully as you can at this present time. When you have done this, bend down and touch your palms to the earth, experiencing the ground beneath you. Feel the great power of the earth connecting to your palms. Again close your eyes and breathe and feel the experience fully. When you feel complete, leave your offering on the land, and thank the spirits for your life.

Now sit down on the earth and close your eyes and breathe and simply experience yourself. You might find that a song comes to you, or a dance comes to you, or nothing comes to you—just experience the moment.

We give Thanks to the earth
We give Thanks
    under the apple tree
We give Thanks
    at sunrise and sunset
Over blue waters
        we give Thanks
With tobacco
        we give Thanks
With blue corn
        we give Thanks
Our Souls are coming
        over mountains
Over rainbows of light
on the breath of tigers
            our souls are coming
We give back the souls we have taken,
    take back the souls we have given away
Gathering them up in our arms
We give Thanks
            for our souls
            for our children
                we give Thanks
                    —Ellen Jaffe Bitz

CHAPTER 11

PREPARING FOR YOUR OWN SOUL'S RETURN

If you dream it, you can do it.
—Walt Disney

This chapter includes some exercises that will prepare you for supporting your own soul's journey. Doing any kind of journey or meditation can help create great changes in your life if your psyche is working with you rather than against you. To have the support of body, mind, and spirit in moving on with your life, sometimes you must ask for help.

Almost everyone is aware of the power that our dreams hold for us. Dreams provide a key for unlocking some of the richness and complexity of our own unconscious. Besides an understanding of the psyche, our dreams can offer a chance to ask for its help.

There is a way to make your dreams work for you. Before you do each of the exercises in this chapter, program yourself as you go to sleep the night before. Get comfortable under the covers. Feel your head on the pillow, and take a few deep breaths. Now say to yourself, "Tomorrow I will be doing an exercise that will help me be more creative in my life. I ask for help from my unconscious, that we can work together in preparing my entire being during the night, so that I may be open to a successful experience tomorrow."

A major part of integrating my own soul retrieval has involved writing this book. To pursue and follow through on this extensive and sometimes overwhelming project, I have made an incredible leap in consciousness. In this chapter you can come along on some of my own journeys to see what I have learned along the way: how to work with my attitude and beliefs, how to work in partnership with the spirits, and how to connect with myself enough to be able to "close my thick ears and open my thin ears"[1] to create something beautiful in my life.

I am the type of person who can teach only through my own experience. I love to teach more than I love to do anything else, and because of this I have had to experience the blocks, the problems, and the internal and external demons we all must face in our life's journeys. I hope in this chapter you can learn from my experience how you can try to create a path for yourself.

This chapter is written especially to help those who want to work at a deeper level. Maybe you are not quite ready to explore shamanism yet. Perhaps you are not ready to have a soul retrieval. This chapter contains some tools to prepare you for your own soul's return and can make a difference in your life even if you decide to go no further with shamanism or a soul retrieval.

If you feel you have come far on your own soul's journey, you can always skip the rest of chapter 11. But if your life isn't going as well as it could be, read it through, and maybe you will find one or more missing pieces here. Or maybe the whole chapter will be profound for you.

If you have already been working with shamanism and the shamanic journey, I will suggest ways to journey to your own power animal to ask for help. If you do guided meditations in your own life, you might create your own based on the purpose of each exercise. If you've never practiced with these techniques, feel free to use the exercises I suggest here.

You might find that you want to be in the safety of your own home as you do these exercises. Find a time when you can be alone and quiet. Or you may be more comfortable reading the exercises and then taking a walk to let whatever comes emerge as you move. Moving meditation is a real avenue of creativity, and if you've never done this, I would suggest you try it. Many people find walking, driving, or even taking a shower to be great for letting creative solutions flow.

Don't forget to use the exercise that began the book if "mind chatter" begins to sabotage your experience. Ask yourself if this happens when your mind is telling you the truth, or a lie. If your mind is being honest, try to access that place deep inside yourself where truth comes from. If you get a signal that your mind is lying to you, thank it for its opinion and continue with the work.

RITUALS AND EXERCISES

Returning a Stolen Soul

In tribal societies soul stealing was done on a conscious level. In times when the concept of power-over was part of our evolution, soul stealing was a method of psychic warfare. Today soul stealing continues, though usually at an unconscious level. Why do people participate in this type of theft? Perhaps they want another person's power, energy, or light. Maybe they are jealous or want to maintain a connection with another person. The list of reasons can go on and on. The bottom line here is that one person cannot use another's soul as a source of power, energy, light, or love. In fact, one cannot use someone else's soul for any purpose.

I believe we all participate in soul taking and soul giving on some level, and we do it for a variety of reasons. But the results are the same: the taker is burdened with unusable energy that slows down his or her process, and the one who lost the soul is missing a source of vitality. By the time you have read this far, you know what the consequences of soul loss are. If while reading this book you got a strong feeling you have someone's soul, don't move to a place of despair. The task is not to sit in self-judgment. If you're not sure whether you have someone's soul and want to check it out so you can be fully released, I will offer suggestions on that, too. The first step is to see whether you do hold someone's soul. If you find this is true, please do not judge yourself too harshly. The point here is to heighten your awareness and to act as a responsible person on this planet that is our home.

If you know how to journey, make a short visit to your power animal and ask whether you have someone's soul. If you don't know how to journey, sit or lie down and take a few deep breaths to center yourself. Using the opening exercise of chapter 1 to establish truth or lie, go inside yourself and ask whether you have someone else's soul. You will know the answer on a deep level if you do. Let a yes or no come up. After the answer emerges, check it out. Experience all the body feelings that come with that answer, and see whether this is a response to truth or lie. Take your time; remember to breathe. Breathing is our life force moving. To ascertain intuitive information, it is important to keep your energy flowing. Continue working on this question until you have a clear answer. If the answer is no, don't worry about doing the rest of this exercise; just read on for your own education.

After demonstrating that you are, indeed, holding onto someone's soul, ascertain whose soul you have, either by journeying or by going inside yourself. If you are using shamanic journeying, again visit your power animal and ask whose soul you have. If at this point you don't have a spiritual method for retrieving your own information, sit or lie down and just become quiet. Or you might prefer going outside and taking a walk. You can even try taking a shower or a bath. Maybe there's something else you do for creative problem-solving. Whatever method you use, breathe deeply and ask yourself, "Whose soul am I holding on to?" Don't rush; take whatever time you need for this. If you don't find an answer one day, try again the next. You might find one time of day is clearer than another for this step. Maybe the morning is a better time, before all the distractions of the world come in to cloud you. Or try doing this in that relaxed state right before you drift off to sleep. Sometimes exercising or doing some other activity might stimulate inner guidance. I find some wonderful revelations come to me while I am sweeping or vacuuming or mopping.

Often just acknowledging that you have someone else's soul is enough to release it and send it back. In my training workshops teaching soul retrieval, I ask people to journey and explore this issue. I suggest they ask a power animal for a simple ritual to give the soul back. I stress "simple" because some of the most powerful rituals I have participated in were short and to the point. Remember, intention is the key to ritual. Feel free to do a longer, more complicated ritual; however, a complex ritual is not required to "get the job done." Throughout this entire process, remember to remain in a state of compassion for yourself and all involved in this deed.

Now that you know whose soul you are holding onto, the next step is giving it back. The person whose soul you have can be alive or deceased; this process will work in either case. Journey to your power animal and simply ask for a ritual to give back the soul. Or if you are using your own inner guidance for information, choose a way that has worked for you in getting information. Ask for a ritual you can use to send a soul back. You might also want to try asking for a dream for the same purpose.

If using ritual seems overwhelming and you don't know how to proceed, I will share some of the ways to release a soul that have come from other people's journeys.

- Go out in nature and find a stick. Break the stick, releasing any unnatural hold you might have on someone else.

- Many people have used quartz crystals for giving back a soul in a variety of ways: take a quartz crystal that is dear to you, or buy one; visualizing the person, blow the soul into the crystal. Some people are told to give the crystal to the person as a gift. One person was told to give the crystal to her daughter to sleep with it under her pillow for ten nights. One of my students shared the following method: hold a crystal in your hand; look at it; visualize the person (or feel the person, get in touch with the person); and speak directly to the stolen soul, saying, "(Name's) soul, go home to (name), you don't belong here by me, you belong to (name). So—go home—bless you!" That's it!

- Take any objects you have in your possession belonging to that person, and send them back to the owner.

- Build a small sage fire. Put a piece of sage in the fire for each soul piece you have, saying, "I release you. Return to the one you belong to." When all the pieces of sage have burned, put the fire out with water, and scatter the ashes outside.

- Use breath work. As you inhale, think of the person you are sending to. When you exhale, purposely send the soul back.

- Give the person a gift that might be a representation of the soul to you.

- My favorite method is to call the person on the phone and during the conversation simply blow the person's soul into the phone. (This gives "reach out and touch someone" new meaning.)

These are just some suggestions that you can try if your own ritual hasn't come to you yet. You can also use these as guidelines and change them to make them your own. The true power of ritual is not what you do but having your heart in it.

I am astounded by the results people report to me after doing this process. They have received feedback themselves from the recipient of the soul that some shift happened in their life or energy. The recipients very rarely knew what the person was doing; they knew only that something was different. Here is one story I received:

> During this journey I traveled to the Lower World. As I went through the tunnel, I found myself dawdling as if I didn't want to really reach the other end . . . . I knew what I would find at the other end—that, yes, I was a soul thief, and that I didn't want to give back the soul part I was holding.
>
> Eventually I did reach the far end of the tunnel, and my power animal, the wolf, came in to the end of the tunnel, grabbed my clothing in his teeth, and pulled me out into the Lower World. Then he grabbed me more firmly in his teeth and whirled me around in a spinning circle so fast that I became disoriented. I knew he was doing this on purpose to confuse me and to get me out of my rational mind.
>
> Then, another of my power animals, the hawk, suddenly flew in, landed on my head, and plucked out my eyes. I felt some terror at this but remained still. Then the hawk, taking my two eyes, gave

me his and told me that he did this so that I could see more clearly.

Then my mind ran through a long list of people that I know—alive and dead. The only piece of soul that I had belonged to Joe. He was a former lover of mine, now a very close friend. Looking through the hawk's eyes, I knew that I did have a piece of his soul.

Then the message came that to return it I had to blow the soul part into one of my favorite crystals—or maybe an appropriate rock that I would find—and then I was to give this object to him with the soul part in it. I was not to tell him what it was, just that it was a present from me and a special crystal for him. The message was very strong that I should give him his soul part back in this specific crystal, even though some other rock might work as well.

When the journey was over I thought about giving him this crystal, and I decided to journey again on some other method of returning his soul part, because I did not want to give up this crystal. Although I had been given an option in this journey, it seemed unfinished. I also decided to see if I could find an "appropriate" rock on the beach, but I could not find one that seemed right.

Upon returning home, I looked at the crystal that I had been shown as the one I should use to return his soul part to him. This crystal is an unusual one that has six completely symmetrical sides in a unique configuration. I felt that I was not willing to use it, so that meant I had to find another that I could use to carry his soul part back to him.

I decided again to do a future journey to find an alternative object that I could use to return his soul part.

In a following journey, I journeyed instead to learn what, if any, options I had in the method I could use to return this soul part. During this journey I was given several options, even though there was still a strong message to use the specific crystal that I had been shown previously.

I was going to see Joe on Wednesday night following my journey, in a class. Because we usually spent time together after the class talking over a cup of coffee and a bit of food, I decided Wednesday would be a good time to return this long-held soul part. Meanwhile I had three days to decide what I would use as the transmitter.

Tuesday evening I found a small, polished smoky quartz "egg," heavy with beautiful copper rutilations. Now, this struck my imagination as the perfect vehicle for the soul part transfer. Joe was partial to smoky quartz; an egg is symbolic of new life; and rutile in a crystal is an enhancer of energy.

The polished smoky quartz egg felt right, and I purchased it. At home that evening, I did a drumming and rattling ritual and blew the soul part into the crystal egg. I then placed it in a small red cloth bag that Joe had given me at the time of the Chinese New Year stuffed with a gift. The now "fertile" egg fit perfectly in the small red bag, as if the bag had been made for it.

Wednesday after class, Joe and I and another friend went to a nearby restaurant. I had decided to give the crystal egg to him at the end of the evening and to suggest that he hold it in his hand

for a minute or so when he was alone at home later that evening.
Earlier I had told him that I had a gift for him.

As the three of us were sitting at the table chatting and eating,
he suddenly asked me what I had for him. I took the red bag
from my purse and handed it to him, saying, "I have something
I want to return to you. Here is the red bag you gave me at
Chinese New Year, with a gift in it for you." Then I asked him
to hold it in his hand when he was alone later at his home.

Joe took the red bag and held it in his hand for a moment. Then
he laid it on the table. Curiosity got the better of him, and he slid
the crystal egg from the bag into his hand. He closed his hand
around it, and after a few seconds, while holding it, he became
very emotional. Tears came to his eyes, and he said that he felt
that something had been transferred from the egg to him—some
energy of some sort—and that he was overwhelmed by what he
was feeling. He was visibly shaken by the experience. Then he
put the egg back into the red bag and laid it on the tabletop. He
was almost unable to speak. Then he made the comment that he
felt some need to "integrate with himself the energy he had just
experienced." A few minutes later he slid the crystal egg out of its
red bag again and, holding it in his hand, experienced again the
same strong emotion as tears filled his eyes.

The next morning he called me to tell me that after he got home,
he again held the crystal egg and experienced the same sensa-
tions. That was three times that he felt the energy of the returned
soul part. And unbeknownst to him, I had blown the soul part
into the crystal egg with three breaths. This ex–soul thief cannot
imagine a more successful return of a stolen soul part!

Not all these journeys will have the same dramatic effect, but this report makes a very powerful statement. Don't question your work if you do not obtain the same results. This work can be very subtle, and the reported results vary on how tuned in to self the other person is. Just know you did a courageous thing both in allowing yourself to be more of who you are and in releasing another to follow his or her own soul's journey.

Congratulate yourself! Do something good for yourself. Feel the release, experience yourself, and notice any changes. Again, these changes might be very subtle and may occur over time. Fill yourself up with just you.

Keep looking for any other pieces of soul you might have and continue over time to give them back. Returning a soul is a wonderful way to work on your own wholeness. In a dream I once received the message, "The greatest gift one can give another person is that of free will and choice." You just gave a very great gift.

Feeling Overwhelmed Contacting Your Own Lost Child

Sometimes when we listen to others' stories, our own stories begin to emerge, causing us to experience a range of feelings. There can be great relief as the missing pieces of our own puzzle start to fall into place. Relief also comes when an unseen problem is identified. We may feel fear, however, as our own inner child wakes up. The child that lives inside might emerge with his or her own story, and the child's fear can be experienced by the adult.

As you read this book, you may become overwhelmed by feelings, or you might make contact with your own lost child who is outside yourself. Know that right now you have the tools to handle what is happening. Just take a minute to breathe and experience yourself and the feelings coming up. Keep breathing deeply and slowly. If you don't, the feelings might intensify. Go inside yourself, and ask the frightened (or sad, angry, or lost) voice to speak to you. Listen to his or her story.

Again take a moment to center yourself, continuing to concentrate on your breath. And now remember how old you are today. Contact that adult part. Your adult knows how to take care of your child, to comfort and protect it. Remember what year you are currently in. Remind yourself that the voice of the child is talking about the past, not the present. Bring yourself to present time. Think about and reach way down inside yourself for the tools and the knowledge you have as an adult to comfort your child. There is no need to get stuck back in the feelings of the past. It is important to acknowledge them, but remember that as an adult, you have different choices available to you than you did as a child. Explain this to your child, and comfort your child. Life is different now, so assure your child you are working on creating a good and safe life for yourself.

This is a wonderful opportunity for you to begin to take an adult stance and use the knowledge you have acquired throughout your life. Changing your stance to present time, bringing yourself up to date, to the person you are now, will give you a whole new outlook on yourself—who and where you are and the choices available to you right now.

By speaking to your own lost child you start to establish the lines of communication needed to bring your child home again and to assure the child it is safe to come home now.

Connecting with Oneself

When we are depressed and can't connect to our emotions, we are disconnected from ourselves and our life force, which knows only how to flow. If we are disconnected from ourselves, we cannot be creative in our own lives. We try to keep ourselves numbed out, to find external things that give us a false sense of happiness and security instead of finding what our own inner being is really seeking.

First, set up your space so that the environment around you supports your meditation. Light a candle, or burn some incense that smells pleasant to you. Consider disconnecting your phone so your time alone is not disturbed. You could wear your favorite piece of clothing or put on colors that are pleasing and calming. Find a comfortable place to sit or lie down that supports your going into the deepest part of yourself that you can access at this time.

Close your eyes and take a few deep breaths to center yourself. Experience your surroundings. Feel the air around you. Pay attention to what is happening in your body. Notice places that feel tight or heavy or painful. Where do you feel the least amount of tension? Where do you feel the best in your body right now? Continue to breathe.

Pick a place in your body that feels tense or choose a spot that feels light. And with your breath go to that place; keep breathing, and just simply experience that place. Don't make any judgments about your feelings. No one person—even you—can invalidate your feelings. Feelings *are,* and just experiencing them is the key to transforming their energy. Don't resist or judge what comes up, or the feeling will only expand in order to be experienced.

Closing your "thick ears" and opening your "thin ears," listen to your own inner voice, the voice that is one with the spirit of all life. Let the feeling you are tracking in your body have a voice, and listen to it.

Continue to listen, using your breath like a rope to journey deeper inside yourself. Ask the voice inside what it is you need to do for yourself right now. Ask how it can assist you right now in meeting that need. Next ask the voice to tell you a small step that you can take today or tomorrow that can bring you closer to meeting that need. Now use body cues to determine whether the information you just received is a truth or a lie. Continue breathing to track your feelings; follow as many as you are curious about or have time for today. Realize that under all the feelings you experience there are other feelings, whether positive or problematic, that are being masked.

If you want to look at this issue by journeying, set your intention clearly. Go to your power animal and ask for a way to connect with yourself on a deeper level.

Just as there are many territories in nonordinary reality, there are many inside ourselves. Sometimes in our emotional journey we experience a light place where the feelings are great. Sometimes we find ourselves moving through a dark territory full of feelings of sadness, anger, pain, or hurt. Don't get stuck. Stand up and walk. Keep moving. Life is constant change and movement. If you're willing to move, you can travel through the darkness to the light. Don't attach to where your journey takes you inside yourself. Learn to listen inside, experience the feelings, learn from the feelings, and when you feel ready, move on.

As you continue to do this, you might actually start to discover a map of who you are and where you can access internal strength, compassion, pleasure, intention, intuition, and connection with the earth. Because each person is unique, you must look to yourself to discover the place inside of you, a place where you can find the tools to keep you connected and listening to the information that can help you create and move forward on your own soul's journey.

Belief and Attitude

After a few months of writing *Soul Retrieval,* I found a negative voice inside me chattering away. "You don't know how to write." "Nobody wants to hear what you have to say." "You're lying to the American public." "Who do you think you are, anyway?" I felt I was going crazy.

So I decided to journey and go to my power animal and teacher in nonordinary reality to ask for assistance. First, I went to my power animal, who immediately sent me to the Upper World to meet my teacher. So I went to Isis, my teacher in nonordinary reality who has been helping me write this book. I went to where she lives and said to her, "I can't write the book." To my horror, instead of the comforting, nurturing assistance I had expected, her response was, "That's fine. We'll find someone else to write it. This book *will* be published." Shocked, I looked up at her as I took in this information. The spirits are pretty smart and know how to "cut through the crap" to get us moving. And I'm sure you can guess what my reaction was.

"Wait, wait, give me another chance. I'll try again." After that it was "back to the drawing board." I had no one to feel sorry for me, so I had to either reach inside myself for tools to keep moving or else forfeit the work that was so dear to my heart.

What it all came down to was my beliefs and my attitudes that continued to sabotage my creativity. Earlier in the book I spoke of needing to be able to have intention and to imagine or envision what we want. Another key to creativity is our belief and attitude that we get what we want; the driving force of our belief and attitude can either propel us closer to the goal or pull us back from it.

My next step was doing mental calisthenics. I felt as if someone had thrown me into a gym and put me on a program of lifting weights beyond my capability. But my intention was clear, and my heart was in it. My spirit was cheering me on. Now my mind had to do the work. I had to ask it to start "lifting weights." What did that mean?

Whenever my mind brought forth the inner voice or old messages such as "I can't," and "You're not good enough," I had to "lift" it. This voice had grown so strong! It had been exercising itself for thirty-eight years. So the weakling part of my mind—the part that says "I can and I will and this is important stuff"—had to lift the other, stronger voice out of the way. Slowly and patiently the lifting occurred every day until it became easier.

At that same time a friend sent me a book, *The Magic of Believing,* in which I read story after story of how people became more creative in their lives by changing their beliefs. I was definitely motivated by knowing that people before me had been successful with altering their attitude.

The results were good in many ways. As I learned how to focus my belief and attitude about myself to help with my writing, that change translated to other areas of my life. I discovered that when there was anything in my life I wanted to create or change, establishing a clear intention and believing in myself made the task—and my life—a lot easier. I let go of the inner destructive forces that were weighing me down. I didn't "kill" that part of myself. Instead I transformed the negative energy that had held me back into something positive and creative. I exercised my energy to work with me rather than against me.

I must admit that when you choose to work on your belief and attitude, you are taking a huge risk. What if it doesn't work? Believing "I can't" or "it will never happen" is safe. But nothing happens. You create a place of stagnation, where you can justify saying, "I was right. I knew it would never work." Taking the risk is scary. What if you take the chance, and it doesn't work; will you be crushed and devastated?

I believe that holding a negative attitude prevents your getting what you want. If I change my attitude and "go for it" and then it doesn't work, I'm still at the same place I started. So I might as well try in case it works. It is a risk, but every change we make in our lives involves risk. That's the bottom line.

What are some of the beliefs and attitudes holding you back? In identifying them, it might be helpful to actually write a list of all the reasons you can't do something or have what you want. Or go inside yourself and ask what belief it is that you need to let go of right now.

Notice throughout the following week how much you hear yourself think about or tell others the reasons you can't do something. Slowly change that voice. Clarify for yourself what you are seeking. Whenever that negative voice comes up, immediately make a positive statement to counter it. For example, if the voice says, "I don't have the resources to do this," follow with the statement, "I know I do have the resources for this, and I ask my mind, my heart, and my spirit to help me."

Another way to help yourself in this process is to journey to your power animal. Ask, "What are the beliefs holding me back from my own creativity at this point in time?" A second question for another journey would be, "How do I change or work with these beliefs?"

Our minds are truly a wonderful tool, and most of us are wasting a magnificent source of energy while we indulge in our morbidity. To turn this around, try asking your mind to be a partner in your creativity, and give it an assignment of something positive you are trying to create. If the mind isn't given an assignment, it will just sit and replay all the old negative messages from the past. Try giving it fuel to support your life, and watch what happens.

Intention and Commitment to Life

Shortly after I started the practice of shamanic journeying, my power animal told me that I was living with one foot in this world and one foot in death, not really sure that I wanted to be here. He said I had to make a choice to live or die; I could not continue living split between the two worlds. It took me years to understand fully what my power animal was trying to show me. But as long as I wasn't sure I wanted to live, what I created in my life couldn't truly support life. I have discussed this point earlier.

A few years ago one of my teachers in nonordinary reality gave me a very simple ritual to help with this issue. She told me to go out every day to a spot in nature and leave an offering of corn-meal or tobacco on the earth while consciously giving thanks for my life.

Think about something you can leave on the earth as you give thanks for your own life. Or, if you prefer, as soon as you wake up in the morning, give thanks for your own life. No matter how you feel, even if you are sad or tired or sick in some way, give thanks every day for your life.

Notice whether you start to attract life-giving situations to yourself. Notice what resistances come up for you in choosing life. But make a choice. The universe gives us what we ask for. If we ask for life, we find that life comes. Watch whether the exercise works for you as it did for me.

If you want to journey on this question you can try asking, "How can I make a full commitment to life?"

Are You Ready?

As you experience these exercises, you may find that the issue of readiness appears. Are you ready to be whole? Are you ready to receive life-giving and positive situations and people in your life? Are you ready to change your attitude? And most important, are you ready to let go of your pain? If you are not ready, that's all right. Don't push yourself.

If you're not ready, your intention may not be strong enough to move you forward. Instead of resisting the "I'm not ready" response, try experiencing the fears, the beliefs, the whole range of feelings that are emerging for you. Go inside and ask yourself what is one tiny step that you can take tomorrow to help you become ready. You can also ask this question in a journey to your power animal.

Please remember that taking small steps to climb mountains will get you there just as surely as taking giant leaps. And the small steps will also allow you to climb the mountain consciously as well as in your own comfort range, keeping you in a state of balance and harmony with yourself.

I encourage you just to check in with yourself occasionally to ask about your readiness to let go of your pain and be whole.

The Return to Nature

Nature has so much to teach and is constantly communicating with us. We can turn to the trees, the rocks, the animals, the water, the fire, the wind, the air for all kinds of revelations in our lives. When Michael Harner was learning shamanism with the Conibo Indians in the Upper Amazon, he was told to go sit with a particular "power tree." According to the Conibo, such direct learning from nature is superior to learning from another shaman.

In the shamanic worldview everything is alive. If you are curious about doing this exercise, let me suggest a way.

Take a walk somewhere in nature. If you live in a city, go to your favorite park. Pick a place where you will be safe. Notice whether there is a tree that attracts your attention. From a shamanic point of view, it is possible that the tree is picking *you* by attracting your attention. It can't just shout out, "Hey you—come here!" It calls to you in another way.

Sit down by the tree, asking its permission first. You will know if it's all right. Feel the earth beneath you. Close your eyes, relax, and breathe away all your tensions and cares. Take your time; don't rush. Really ground yourself, experiencing your connection with the earth. Feel yourself being solid and at the same time fluid and connected with all life. Connect with the tree and experience it. Notice whether you can melt into tree consciousness and experience what it feels like to be a tree. Experience how the energy comes up from the earth through the root system to feed the cells in the trunk, the branches, the leaves, the fruits, and the blossoms. The energy might be released by dropping the leaves that are no longer alive or letting go of some beautiful fruit. Notice how the branches grow toward the light, reaching for the sun, reaching toward life. We humans are very similar to trees in that respect. In a dream I was once told, "Life is just the seeds of the light." We also reach to the sun for life.

Introduce yourself to the tree. Ask the tree if it has messages or guidance for you at this time. Close your "thick ears" and open your "thin ears." The message will come by direct revelation. You might feel the answer in your heart, solar plexus, or abdomen, or you might hear it telepathically. Maybe you will get a vision; perhaps you might smell something different. Open all your senses to how the information is coming. The information might come in a combination of the ways I mentioned. Keep speaking silently to the tree until you feel complete. Thank the tree for communicating, helping, and teaching you. You might feel moved to ask the tree if it needs something from you. You may wish to leave an offering or a gift to the earth, the trees, and the helping spirits.

You can continue this practice at various times, speaking with any parts of nature you care to, being with a river or an ocean or any body of water, sitting with a rock, sitting or walking with and communicating with any of the elements. These aspects of nature have been here a very long time. They have much wisdom to impart to us about ourselves as well as about how we can create healing for the earth, our home.

EPILOGUE

It was out of the dynamic of cosmic celebration that
we were created in the first place. We are to become
celebration and generosity, burst into self-awareness.
What is the human? The human is a space, an
opening, where the universe celebrates its existence.
—*Brian Swimme,* The Universe is a Green Dragon

Practicing shamanism involves understanding the concept of power and the right use of power. Power is the ability to transform any energy. When we are whole and in our power, the possibilities for what we can do are endless.

A few years ago my power animal came to me in a journey and said, "One day you will write a book called *The Art of the Wizard,* which will be about the water situation in this country." At that time (as well as now) I was quite concerned about how we have polluted our sources of water and was worried about the quality of our existing water. I had my B.A. in biology, specializing in marine biology, so I thought this message meant I had to return to school and get my master's degree in marine biology. I started to investigate this possibility. In some ways I was terrified to think I had to enter into the school system again, but I felt if this were the next step on my path, I would find the courage and strength to pursue it.

As I was considering what to do, I taught a workshop on shamanism in Tucson, Arizona. In the workshop one participant introduced himself as a chemist for the water department. During the lunch break I seized the opportunity to speak with him, and I shared my journey. He looked at me and said, "Sandy, shamans for centuries have been restoring balance to the environment. Science is not going to figure out this problem. Continue on your spiritual path. This is where the answer lies." I felt that he was right and was grateful for our conversation. I realized that the Native American communities may provide answers and guidance for our environmental dilemmas. Just one example is the way the Hopi have been able to make rain when it is needed.

A year later, while assisting Michael Harner in a workshop, I journeyed when the group intention was to find a lost ritual for healing. In my journey I met a very old dolphin lying on a huge rock in the middle of the sea. This dolphin was ancient and appeared to be from the very beginning of time. He said to me, "The one gift that man has that no other animal has is the ability to pass light through his hands." He told me to put my hands over any water I was drinking and allow with intention the light of the universe to pass through my hands to create pure drinking water for myself.

You might want to try this. Before drinking a glass of water or eating your food, bless the water or food by holding your hands over it. Keep your hands there for thirty seconds to one minute, and allow the light to come through your hands. Notice as you drink and eat whether you feel any subtle differences in yourself or your feelings about the act of blessing.

M y own readiness to pursue this information on healing the environment was a little before its time. I have gone slowly, step by step, as I deepen my own understanding of the healing process.

MIRRORING

There's a metaphysical principle dealing with the relationship of the microcosm and macrocosm that says, "As above, so below. As within, so without." These words speak to the aspect of mirroring. Let me give you an example. I might wake up in the morning feeling very angry. I get dressed and get into my car and go to town. Someone in a great rush honks at me in the car behind, yelling obscenities at me. I get to town and go to the store, where the clerk is mean to me. My external world begins to mirror what I am feeling internally.

Let's take this concept one step further. If we as human beings have lost our souls, could it be that we are having that mirrored back to us by our environment? Are we living on a planet that has lost its soul? Perhaps the environmental problems we are seeing today reflect our own soul loss. Are the diseases we are seeing today mirroring back to us how the planet has lost its soul?

Consider the immune deficiency diseases that afflict us in epidemic proportions: the blood is the waterway of our bodies. We are also dealing with problems of water pollution on the earth. Is there any relationship?

Going on the theory of "the hundredth monkey," I wonder whether bringing back a significant number of souls will help to recover the soul of the earth, mirroring back to us our return to harmony.

If you are an explorer of metaphysics, you might want to follow me on an expansion of this theory. Many survivors of near-death experiences report going to a great blinding light that pulsates only love. In my own near-death experience in 1971, I, too, was received by the light. For me, this light represented the Father and Mother God. I started thinking about God's being pure light. The Bible says that God created man in his own image. What that means to me, then, is that we are really balls of light. I started to experience myself as being light surrounded by matter, the body. We are a body; we have a mind; and we have this beautiful light that shines in us that is Spirit, which connects us to the divine.

Many of us feel as though we are cut off from the spiritual aspect of ourselves. We feel isolated from the source. When we embark on a spiritual path, however, we can reconnect with the light that shines within us. We no longer have to seek the light outside ourselves. When we reconnect with Spirit, the ego quiets; our boundaries and defenses let down; and we can experience what it feels like to be part of life and connected to the whole. We lose the sense of being separate from any living being but feel ourselves being the air, the water, the earth, the fire, the animals, the trees, the plants, the insects, and the rocks. We experience a oneness with our friends and our enemies. We connect with the spirit that moves in all things. We can now tap into the universal flow and find we have the strength and power we need for healing.

RETRIEVING THE PLANET'S SOUL

How can we use this energy in a right way rather than a destructive way? We can continue working on a personal level as I have described in this book. We can also begin to work on a broader level. Traditional shamans didn't work only with the diseases of human beings. Mircea Eliade suggests,

> *Since sickness is interpreted as a flight of the soul, cure involves calling it back. Shamans implore the patient's soul to return from the distant mountains, valleys, rivers, forests and fields, or wherever it may be wandering. The same summoning back of the soul is found among the Karen of Burma who, in addition, employ a similar treatment for the "sickness" of the rice imploring its "soul" to return to the crop. The same commonly is used by the Chinese.[1]*

Shamans in other cultures perform soul retrieval ceremonies for the crops.

The Bare'e Toradja of Celebes have women or men who pose as women who are known as the *bajasa*. Their particular technique consists of journeys to the sky or underworld. The *bajasa* climbs the rainbow to the house of Pue di Songe, Supreme God, to bring back the soul of the patient. She also seeks and brings back the "soul of the rice" when it deserts the crops, causing them to wither and die.[2] Among the Dyak of Borneo the men usually do personal healing, whereas the women are specialists in the "treatment" of paddy harvests and do soul retrievals for the crops.[3]

I hope we can learn from these Southeast Asian and Oceanic societies as well as from other cultures. We can do soul retrievals for the land that has been traumatized by nuclear radiation or chemical pollution. We can do soul retrievals for polluted water and for land where forests have been mowed down.

I think we all have visited places on the planet where we just "feel" the place has no soul. This means this place has lost its vitality, its life force and energy. We can use what we know about soul retrieval to create a healing ritual. If you know how to journey, you can ask in your journeying how to do a soul retrieval for the earth, the water, the air. If you don't practice journeying, reach into your heart to find a ritual or ceremony for healing. Remember that the keys are intention or purpose, putting your heart into the work, commitment to what you are doing, and trusting that the healing will come. When we do choose to work in this way, we must be responsible to the environment once the healing is accomplished.

REMEMBER THE CIRCLE

If we are going to live on this planet and truly celebrate life, then it is time to come home. Before I teach a soul retrieval workshop, I journey to ask for guidance on my teaching; I get the same response in every journey. My power animal always says, "Remember, this is a celebration!"

Let's take the energy we have created in this book to create a circle. Imagine being a part of a great planetary circle committed to life and wholeness. Imagine joining hands with others like you who are seeking wholeness and healing for their own selves and others. Feel the power that comes from joining hands with like-minded people. If you can't yet feel it, imagine it. Know that, step by step, we are working on a wonderful healing journey for all life. You are now part of an unseen circle, a circle of love held together by people and helping spirits. Know the circle is supporting you on your own soul's journey. Please take from the power of the circle when you need to, and give back to it when you have some extra to give. Know that circles don't end—they continue. This book doesn't end either; the work here continues. Remember if you can dream it, if you can imagine it, you can make it happen.

The Earth wants all her children home so she can come home too, so all of us can participate in partnership in the great celebration called life. Welcome home!

ILLNESS FROM A SHAMANIC PERSPECTIVE

Only the shaman . . ."sees" the spirits and knows
how to exorcise them; only he recognizes that the
soul has fled, and is able to overtake it, in
ecstasy, and return it to its body.
—*Mircea Eliade,* Shamanism:
Archaic Techniques of Ecstasy

In working shamanically with people over the last eleven years I have experienced all aspects of illness from a shamanic perspective. In shamanism we see that all illnesses—emotional, mental, physical, and spiritual—are treated the same. Whatever form it takes, illness is illness and shows disharmony in a person's life.

As Michael Harner points out in *The Way of the Shaman,* one reason a person may become ill is that his or her power animal has gone away and a new one has not come in to replace it. Signs that a person has lost his or her power are chronic health problems, always being ill with a cold or the flu or some other complaint of illness. Chronic depression or suicidal tendencies is another cue that a person may be suffering from a loss of power. Chronic misfortune is yet another cue—perhaps a person falls down the stairs, is then in a car accident, and then has a fire in his or her house. I think we all know someone who has had such a string of bad fortune that it causes us to wonder what is happening. A string of misfortune like this is another indication to me that a client has lost power.

The role of a power animal is to keep a person protected from harm. The power animal also keeps one healthy and well balanced. Most of us don't work regularly with our animals; they might become bored and leave us after a number of years. Usually a new animal will replace the one that left; also, most of us have many animals around us at one time working in our behalf. But a problem occurs when a person loses a power animal, and no replacement appears. The shaman must enter nonordinary reality and look for an old power animal to come back and help. The method for doing this is described in detail in *The Way of the Shaman,* by Michael Harner.[1]

When a person is dealing with a localized illness, such as some forms of cancer or a pain in the shoulder or emotional pain in the heart, there is a good possibility that the person is suffering from a spiritual intrusion. All illness has a spiritual identity. This means that when I journey into a client's body to look at illness, it will actually have an identity. It will look like a fanged reptile, or an insect, or some dark, sludgy material. The illness will show itself in a form that is repulsive to me. Some of the modern work being done with imagery and healing correlates with what shamans have always seen with illness. For example, when patients with cancer draw what their illness looks like, they often draw fanged reptiles and insects. People see on their own what classical shamans have always seen.

It is the role of the shaman to identify the spiritual nature of the illness and its location in the body. Once this is known, the shaman removes the illness by pulling or "sucking" it out of the body. This is called a shamanic extraction.[2]

These spiritual intrusions are spirits misplaced in the person's body—they are not evil spirits. Here's a simple example: If a spider comes into your house, the spider is not evil. It is misplaced, and we hope you will remove the spider and place it outside, back on the earth where it belongs.

In an illness, these intrusions "believe" that the patient's body is home. The shaman removes the intrusion and puts it back into nature again, where it is neutralized. The hard part for the shaman lies in trying to get the intrusion out of the body. The intrusion has a nice, comfortable, warm home and has no intention of leaving. Before I work with intrusions, I want to gather all my power to me by singing and using my rattle, so that I go into the work having more power than this intrusion has. And I must have enough power to shield myself so that the intrusion will not enter into my body.

Spiritual intrusions often enter a person because of negative thought forms. For example, if I am angry at someone and can't express my anger directly, I may send an intrusion to that person, even though I have no intention of doing harm. If the person does not have power at the time, I might unconsciously send illness their way. In populated cities negative thought forms are constantly flying around. Thus, from a shamanic perspective, it is essential for us to keep a connection with our power animal to avoid becoming ill. It is also essential that we learn how to deal with our feelings in a constructive way. *The Way of the Shaman* is a wonderful book to help you learn how to discover and work with your power animals.

Another reason that a person may fall ill is soul loss. The soul may be frightened away, lost, or stolen. Persons who have lost parts of their souls describe themselves as dissociated, and often have no memory of certain segments of their lives. Chronic depression, suicidal tendencies, and chronic illnesses are also symptoms of soul loss. It is emotionally painful to be fragmented, dissociated, and not feeling part of life.

When a person complains to me that he or she has not "been myself" since a trauma, such as surgery, an accident, a divorce, or the death of someone close, I suspect soul loss. Signs of soul loss are discussed more thoroughly in chapter 1.

Let me emphasize that in all of these cases, I am describing partial soul loss. By contrast, a person in a coma is experiencing full soul loss. In coma, the soul may be trying to cross over into death and has become lost, or there may be unresolved issues in ordinary reality that keep the person from making that transition. Perhaps the soul doesn't know how to come back into the body. In any case, the soul loss is complete, and the person is unable to function in ordinary reality.

Traditionally shamans have been people who have had a near-death experience, a life-threatening illness, or a psychotic break. In my case, I almost drowned, and this near-death experience showed me the way to the other side. Shamans are those who have gone to "the other side" and come back to life on their own, bringing back the knowledge of how to make the transition from life to death and then back to life again. In the shamanic literature the term for this person is the *wounded healer*. A shaman can help a dying soul who is lost or confused about how to make the transition by actually guiding the soul either to the light or to a deceased relative who will take it the rest of the way. When a soul wants to reenter the body, a soul retrieval would be called for.

In all the cases of illness I've described, my experience can give me clues to what is happening for a person. But the diagnosis comes from my working with my power animal. In shamanism we never make our own decisions in the work; we work with the power of the universe. In shamanism we never use our own energy or as Loren Smith, a Pomo shaman in Northern California, says, "We never use the energy we are born with."

The first thing I do when a client comes to me for emotional or physical healing is to journey to my power animal and ask what this person needs at this time. Usually I learn that a combination of methods must be used. For example, in working with Mary I saw that there was a spiritual intrusion in her body because she had lost a part of her soul. The universe cannot stand a void, so an intrusion might enter to fill up that space. In a case like this, I would remove the intrusion first and then do a soul retrieval.

With John, my own power animal showed me that John's power animal had left, and he had lost his power. An intrusion had entered his body, so I had to do an extraction first and then a power animal retrieval.

When I worked with Debbie, who was severely traumatized by a rape, my power animal instructed me first to do a power animal retrieval to give Debbie the strength and energy to deal with her trauma. Then I was instructed to do an extraction to remove the intrusion that had formed from the negative energy around her. After that I was instructed to retrieve the lost soul that had been frightened away by the trauma.

Sometimes I am instructed to do just a power animal retrieval, or an extraction, or just a soul retrieval. But I always do a diagnostic journey to ascertain this information.

Shamanic healing is not a "quick fix." It is very common to have to see a client several times to make sure that the work has been completed. I want to know that a person's power animal is vital or that the intrusion is truly gone or that the soul parts needed back at this time are in place in the client's body.

APPENDIX B

SHAMANIC TRAINING WORKSHOPS

As I have emphasized throughout the book, the method of soul retrieval should not be attempted without firsthand training. If you wish to obtain information on training workshops in shamanism and shamanic healing, a schedule of workshops given by me and by my associates at various locations in the United States and elsewhere is available from the following address:

The Foundation for Shamanic Studies
Box 670, Belden Station
Norwalk, CT 06852
Telephone: (203) 454–2825

The Foundation for Shamanic Studies is a nonprofit organization whose work is to preserve, transmit, and apply shamanic knowledge to contemporary problems of the planet.

NOTES

Introduction

    1. Mircea Eliade, *Shamanism: Archaic Techniques of Ecstasy,* trans. Willard R. Trask, Bollingen series, vol. 76, (Princeton, NJ: Princeton Univ. Press, 1972), p. 5.

    2. Michael Harner, *The Way of the Shaman,* 3d ed. (San Francisco: Harper & Row, 1990). Originally published 1980.

Chapter 1: Soul Loss

    1. This exercise was taught to me by Gloria Sherman in a Feminism, Gestalt, Bodywork class in Berkeley, California, in 1980.

    2. Eliade, *Shamanism,* pp. 215–16.

    3. Eliade, *Shamanism,* pp. 326–27

    4. John Bradshaw, *Healing the Shame that Binds You* (Pompano Beach, FL: Health Communications, 1988), p. 75.

    5. Jeanne Achterberg, "The Wounded Healer," from *The Shaman's Path,* by Gary Doore (Boston: Shambhala, 1988), p. 121.

    6. M. L. Von Franz, *Projection and Recollection in Jungian Psychology* (Peru, IL: Open Court, La Salle & Condon, 1980).

Chapter 2: Soul Retrieval

    1. Eliade, *Shamanism,* pp. 216–17.

    2. Harner, *The Way of the Shaman,* p. 29.

    3. Jeanne Achterberg, *Imagery in Healing: Shamanism and Modern Medicine* (Boston: New Science Library/Shambhala, 1985), p. 42.

    4. Maxwell C. Cade and Nona Coxhead, *The Awakened Mind:*

Biofeedback and the Development of Higher States of Awareness (Great Britain: Element Books, 1979), p. 25.

5. Itzhak Bentov, *Stalking the Wild Pendulum* (New York: E. P. Dutton, 1977), p. 30.

6. Eliade, *Shamanism,* p. 420.

7. Eliade, *Shamanism,* pp. 220–21.

8. Harner, *The Way of the Shaman,* pp. 57–65.

9. Eliade, *Shamanism,* pp. 270–71.

10. Harner, *The Way of the Shaman,* pp. 25–30.

11. Sandra Ingerman, "Welcoming Ourselves Back Home: The Application of Shamanic Soul Retrieval in the Treatment of Trauma Cases," *Shaman's Drum,* Midsummer 1989, p. 25.

Chapter 3: Tracking Lost Souls

1. Ingerman, "Welcoming Ourselves Back Home," p. 27.

2. Ingerman, "Welcoming Ourselves Back Home," pp. 27–28.

Chapter 4: A Question of Technique

1. According to a national survey conducted in 1985 by David Finkelhor for the Los Angeles Polling Organization, 277 of the 1,481 women and 167 of the 1,145 men surveyed reported having been sexually abused as children. David Finkelhor, Gerald Hotaling, I. A. Lewis, Christine Smith, "Sexual Abuse in a National Survey of Adult Men and Women: Prevalence, Characteristics and Risk Factors," *Child Abuse and Neglect* 14 (1990): 19–28.

2. G. V. Ksendofotov, quoted in Henri F. Ellenberger, *The Discovery of Dynamic Psychiatry* (New York: Basic Books, 1970), p. 7.

3. Åke Hultkrantz, *The Religion of the American Indians* (Berkeley and Los Angeles: Univ. of California Press, 1979), p. 131.

Chapter 5: Classical Examples of Soul Retrieval

The epigraph was taken from Holger Kalweit's *Dreamtime and Inner Space* (Boston: Shambhala, 1988), p. 21.

1. Joseph Campbell, *The Way of the Animal Powers: Historical Atlas of World Mythology,* vol. 1, Alfred Van der Marck editions (San Francisco: Harper & Row, 1983), p. 176.

2. Eliade, *Shamanism,* pp. 350–51.

3. Charles Nicholl, *Borderlines: A Journey in Thailand and Burma* (New York: Viking Penguin, 1989), pp. 101–11.

Chapter 6: Community

1. Eliade, *Shamanism,* pp. 217–18.

2. Robert Francis Johnson, "Rites of Passage: The Search for Myth and Meaning," *Crosswinds* 2, no. 6 (Aug. 1990): 14.

3. Nicholl, *Borderlines,* p. 235.

Chapter 7: When Souls Have Been Stolen

1. Bradshaw, *Healing the Shame that Binds You,* p. 22.

2. Bradshaw, *Healing the Shame that Binds You,* p. 6.

3. Hultkrantz, *The Religion of the American Indians,* p. 89.

Chapter 11: Preparing for Your Own Soul's Return

1. Margaret Nowak and Stephen Durrant, *The Tale of the Nisan Shamaness: The Manchu Folk Epic* (Seattle: Univ. of Washington Press, 1977). The shamaness keeps saying throughout the text, "Close your thick ears and open your thin ears." To me this line is a great way of saying, "Open to the information that the unseen and subtle realms are giving to you." To make this point I use the Nisan shamaness's line throughout the chapter.

Epilogue

1. Eliade, *Shamanism,* p. 442.

2. Eliade, *Shamanism,* p. 353.

3. Eliade, *Shamanism,* p. 350.

Appendix A: Illness from a Shamanic Perspective

1. Harner, *The Way of the Shaman,* pp. 76–85.

2. Harner, *The Way of the Shaman,* p. 116.

BIBLIOGRAPHY

Achterberg, Jeanne. *Imagery in Healing: Shamanism and Modern Medicine*. Boston: New Science Library/Shambhala, 1985.

————. "The Wounded Healer." In *The Shaman's Path*, by Gary Doore. Boston: Shambhala, 1988.

Berry, Thomas. *The Dream of the Earth*. San Francisco: Sierra Club Books, 1988.

Bradshaw, John. *Healing the Shame that Binds You*. Pompano Beach, FL: Health Communications, 1988.

Bristol, Claude M. *The Magic of Believing*. New York: Pocket Books, Simon & Schuster, 1948.

Cade, Maxwell C., and Nona Coxhead. *The Awakened Mind: Biofeedback and the Development of Higher States of Awareness*. Great Britain: Element Books, 1979.

Campbell, Joseph. *The Way of the Animal Powers: Historical Atlas of World Mythology,* vol. 1. Alfred Van der Marck editions. San Francisco: Harper & Row, 1983.

Campbell, Joseph, with Bill Moyers. *The Power of Myth*. New York: Doubleday, 1988.

Connelly, Dianne M. *All Sickness Is Homesickness*. Columbia, MD: Centre for Traditional Acupuncture, 1986.

Eliade, Mircea. *Shamanism: Archaic Techniques of Ecstasy*. Translated by Willard R. Trask. Bollingen Series, vol. 76. Princeton, NJ: Princeton Univ. Press, 1972.

Ellenberger, Henri F. *The Discovery of the Unconscious: The History and Evolution of Dynamic Psychiatry*. New York: Basic Books, 1970.

Fitzhugh, William W., and Aron Crowell. *Crossroads of Continents: Cultures of Siberia and Alaska.* Washington, DC: Smithsonian Institution Press, 1988.

Harner, Michael. *The Way of the Shaman,* 3d ed. San Francisco: Harper & Row, 1990. Originally published 1980.

Hultkrantz, Åke. *The Religion of the American Indians.* Berkeley & Los Angeles: Univ. of California Press, 1979.

Ingerman, Sandra. "Welcoming Our Selves Back Home: The Application of Shamanic Soul-Retrieval Techniques in the Treatment of Trauma Cases." *Shaman's Drum,* Midsummer 1989, pp.24–29.

Johnson, Robert Francis. "Rites of Passage: The Search for Myth and Meaning." *Crosswinds* 2, no. 6 (1990), p.14.

Kalweit, Holger. *Dreamtime and Inner Space.* Boston: Shambhala, 1988.

Lewis, John Wren. "The Darkness of God—A Personal Report on Consciousness Transformation Through an Encounter with Death." *Journal of Humanistic Psychology* 28, no. 2 (Spring 1988), pp. 105–21.

Nicholl, Charles. *Borderlines: A Journey in Thailand and Burma.* New York: Viking Penguin, 1989.

Nowak, Margaret, and Stephen Durrant. *The Tale of the Nisan Shamaness: The Manchu Folk Epic.* Seattle: Univ. of Washington Press, 1977.

Stones, Bones and Skin: Ritual and Shamanic Art. An Artscanada book. Toronto, Ontario: Society for Art Publications, 1977.

Swimme, Brian. *The Universe Is a Green Dragon.* Santa Fe, NM: Bear & Company, 1984.

Von Franz, M. L. *Projection and Recollection in Jungian Psychology.* Peru, IL: Open Court, La Salle & Condon, 1980.

INDEX

Abandonment, 13, 88, 89, 100, 162

Abuse: generational, 99, 117, 148, 150; and soul loss, 11, 12, 13, 19, 144, 149–50; statistics, 66. *See also* Incest; Sexual abuse

Acceptance, 138

Accidents: as loss of power, 199; soul loss following, 11, 13, 19, 169, 202

Achterberg, Jeanne, 28; "The Wounded Healer," 22

Addiction, 11, 19, 23, 113, 136

Adolescence, 15, 90–91

Adulthood, 161, 163, 165, 169, 184

Africa, shamanism in, 1, 78

Alcohol, 16, 23, 45, 67, 112

Altered states of consciousness, 1, 12, 17, 28, 40. *See also* Drumming

Amazon, shamanism in, 18, 191

Andes, shamanism in, 18, 31

Anger, 54–55, 91; following soul retrieval, 132, 166–68

Asia, shamanism in, 1, 17–18, 85. *See also* China; Central Asia; Southeast Asia

Attitude, 186–89

Australia, shamanism in, 1, 78

Belief, 164, 174; and creativity, 186–89; systems, 2, 3, 163

Bible, the, 195

Blowing: and client vulnerability, 67, 152; illustrated, 75, 76; of power animal, 152; to release a soul, 178, 179, 180, 181; of returned soul parts, 43, 51, 66, 74–75, 95, 102, 107. *See also* Soul parts

Bodily soul, 71

Body sensations, 9, 10

Bodywork, 128, 156, 168

Borneo, soul retrieval in, 80, 197

Bradshaw, John, *Healing the Shame that Binds You,* 19, 112–13

Brain waves, 28–29

Breath work, 165, 178

British Columbia, shamanism in, 30, 31

Burma, soul retrieval in, 196

Buryat shamanism, 79, 85. *See also* Central Asia, shamanism in

Cade, Maxwell, 28–29

Campbell, Joseph, *The Way of the Animal Powers,* 79

Cancer, 22, 200
Candles, 47–48, 68, 93
Cave of the Lost Children, 33, 52–55, 59; illustrated, 53
Celebes, soul retrieval in, 197
Celebration of life, 92, 198
Central Asia, shamanism in, 17–18, 78, 79, 85
Change, after soul retrieval, 67, 128, 132, 143, 151. *See also* Soul retrieval, effects of
Chanting, 81
Chi, 168. *See also* Energy
Child abuse, 37, 65, 148, 150, 208n.1. *See also* Incest; Sexual abuse
Childbirth, 90
Childhood: 3, 15; illness during, 23, 100, 101; lost, 50–52; rejection, 13, 88, 89, 131–32; and soul stealing, 99–100, 111; trauma, 36, 41, 73, 76, 88, 89, 127, 132. *See also* Adulthood; Cave of the Lost Children; Child abuse; Incest; Inner child; Memories
Children, of alcoholic parents, 54, 55
China: shamanism in, 78, 85, 196; tomb art of, 31
Circle technique, 92–95, 197–98
Cities, 85, 201
Client histories, 64–65. *See also* Healer-client relationships
Codependency, 111–13, 144
Coma, 14, 170, 201
Combat experiences, 11, 19, 20, 37, 73, 91
Commitment: to healing, 169, 197; to life, 164–65, 189–90; to therapy, 151
Communication, with retrieved

soul parts, 162–63, 167. *See also* Soul parts, integration of
Community: celebration of life, 92; disintegration of, 85, 88, 150; intentional, 96; religious, 91–92; rites of passage, 89–91; support of, 84–88, 89, 91, 95–96, 169; in traditional shamanism, 84–85. *See also* Soul parts, integration of
Compassion, 177
Conibo Indians, 191
Core shamanism, 40
Crops, soul retrieval ceremonies for, 196–97
Crystals: in Borneo, 80; gifts of, 77, 106; in modern shamanism, 29, 68; in Southeast Asian shamanism, 29; use of, 48, 68, 69, 74, 166, 178; as vehicle for release of soul, 178, 180–82

Death: of a loved one, 12, 14, 23, 31, 104, 105, 202; preoccupation with, following soul retrieval, 128; soul loss as cause of, 22, 113. *See also* Coma; Near-death experiences; Soul stealing
Depression, 18–19, 57, 150, 184; in adolescence, 15, 91; chronic, 14, 23, 128, 135, 164, 199, 201; and energy flow, 161; following soul retrieval, 128, 133, 140, 166
Disorientation, following soul retrieval, 125–26
Dissociation, 19–20, 149–50, 166, 201; defined, 13; and multiple personality disorders, 21, 150
Divorce, 23, 73; as childhood

trauma, 54, 55, 73, 88; and soul
loss, 104, 109, 111–12, 201
Dreams, 10, 173, 177; following
soul retrieval, 128, 143
Dream work, 20, 39
Drugs: and loss of soul, 90, 113;
used in shamanic practice, 1;
used to fill a void, 16, 19, 45
Drumming: to enter Shamanic
State of Consciousness, 28, 40,
42, 50, 69–70, 94; significance
of, 28–29, 79; on tape, 48, 69;
as universal characteristic of
shamanism, 28
Drums, 29, 48, 79
Dyak of Borneo, 80, 197

Eagle, as power animal, 32, 33
Earth: children of, 77, 198; heartbeat of, 29, 34; soul of, 195. *See
also* Planet, health of
Eating disorders, 23, 45, 91, 113,
136, 150, 151, 156
Ego, 160
Eliade, Mircea, 17–18, 28, 30, 31,
78, 80, 196; classification of
nonordinary reality, 34;
*Shamanism: Archaic Techniques
of Ecstasy,* 1, 85–86
Energy: depletion, 15; from the
earth, 192; and power, 193;
following soul retrieval, 103,
107–8, 125, 140; stop of flow,
160–61, 168; used in shamanism, 202
Environmental problems, 136,
194, 195. *See also* Planet, health
of
Exercises: blessing water or food,
194; creating a sense of group
support, 84; experiencing
wholeness, 26–27; heightened

awareness, 126; intention and
trust, 77; learning from nature,
191–92; lighting a candle,
47–48; making your dreams
work for you, 173–74; an offering to the spirits, 171; purpose
of, 5; remembering your own
light, 119; returning a stolen
soul, 175–79; truth or lie? 9,
176, 185. *See also* Ritual
Family: as community, 85; disso-
lution of, 85, 88, 89; nuclear,
85, 88; psychic battles in, 100,
101, 132; relationships, 139,
145–49. *See also* Abuse; Child
abuse; Childhood
Fire, use in ritual, 167, 178
Foundation for Shamanic Studies,
41, 205
Fragmentation, 164–65. *See also*
Dissociation
Free association, 20, 39
Free soul, 71, 114
Freudian psychology, 39

Gambling, 23, 113
Ghosts, in traditional shaman-
ism, 18
Giraffe, as power animal, 153, 156
Great Mother, 48
Growth, 140, 163. *See also*
Change
Guardians, 30, 32–33, 49; in the
Land of the Dead, 114, 115.
See also Helping spirits; Power
animals
Guilt, 132, 145, 149

Harner, Michael, 1, 17, 78; and
Conibo Indians, 191; core
shamanism, 40; Foundation
for Shamanic Studies, 41, 205;

functions of, 32, 200; as guardians, 32, 52–54, 103; help in navigating nonordinary reality, 32, 60, 89; and illness, 199, 200, 201; and the Land of the Dead, 114, 116, 117; loss of, 200; and medicine bags, 29–30; in ordinary reality, 32; personalities of, 32; relationship with, 161–62; telepathic communication with, 41–42, 51; working with, 41, 21. *See also* Guardians; Helping spirits

Power-over, 99, 118, 175

Power places, 33–34, 162

Power song, 50, 69, 93, 154, 201

Pre-Columbian culture, shamanism in, 31

Protection, methods of, 102–3

Psychopomp, 1

Psychotherapy: and abuse, 150; client in, 64; compared to shamanic approach, 20–21, 38–40, 64–65; dissociation in, 19–20, 150; effectiveness of, 11–12, 49–50; Jungian, 22, 39; model of healing in, 39; soul retrieval in, 131–33

Psychotic breaks, 202

Quartz crystals. *See* Crystals

Rape, and soul loss, 19, 20, 37, 141–42, 203. *See also* Incest

Rattle: as shaman's tool, 28, 29, 48, 68; use of, 55, 69, 75, 93, 107, 181, 201

Reality: creating one's own, 163; nature of, 3

Relationships: abusive, 99; and community, 89; effects of soul retrieval on, 137–49, 155–56; guidance on, 35; inability to experience intimacy in, 55, 88, 104; and lost parts, 10, 12–13, 104; right, 143; unhealthy, 12, 52, 143, 144. *See also* Codependency; Family; Marriages

Religion, as community, 91–92

Religious belief, 17

Responsibility, 163, 164, 169

Right-brain functions, 2, 3, 29

Rites of passage, 89–91

Ritual: for connecting with oneself, 184–85; for integration and healing, 165–68, 171, 194, 197; for returning a soul, 175–82; of thanks for one's life, 190. *See also* Exercises

Sage fires, 167, 178

Seance, 80, 86

Self-esteem, 72. *See also* Wholeness

Self-help, and soul retrieval, 87–88

Separation, trauma of, 14, 22, 100. *See also* Death; Divorce

Serpent motif, 30, 31

Sex, addiction to, 19, 23, 113

Sexual abuse, 13, 44, 76, 112, 132, 133, 149; case studies, 150–58; and illness, 157; reporting to clients on, 75–76; and soul loss at puberty, 91, 155; survey on, 208n.1. *See also* Incest; Rape

Sexuality, inhibited, 91

Shaman, role of, 1, 18, 21, 27–28, 63, 86–87, 200

Shaman, tools of, 29–30, 69, 86.
    See also Crystals; Medicine
    bags; Soul catchers
Shamanic cultures, features of,
    17, 40
Shamanic extraction, 200, 203
Shamanic healing, 11, 63–64;
    client in, 64–67. *See also* Soul
    retrieval
Shamanic journey: diagnostic,
    203; explained, 70–71; illus-
    trated, 70, 74; to the Land of
    the Dead, 115–17; metaphor
    in, 75; to one's own power ani-
    mal, 174–75; sharing the expe-
    rience with clients, 75–77. *See
    also* Lower World; Middle
    World; Upper World
Shamanic State of Conscious-
    ness, 28, 40
Shamanic worldview, 20, 191
Shamanism: dismissed, 64, 134;
    and near-death experiences,
    195, 202; opening to, 48; tradi-
    tional, 11, 17, 18, 36, 38, 48,
    65–66, 78–82, 85, 196–97;
    universal characteristics of, 28.
    See also Soul retrieval, tradi-
    tional means of
Shamans, near-death experiences
    of, 195, 202
Shock, 13
Siberia, shamanism in, 1, 18, 30,
    78
Sisiutl, 30, 31
Sleep disorders, 57, 58, 157
Smith, Loren (Pomo shaman),
    202
Social problems, 87
Soul: belief regarding, 71; de-
    fined, 11

Soul catchers, 30, 48, 68, 69, 166;
    illustrated, 30, 31. *See also*
    Crystals
Soul loss: during adolescence,
    90–91; ancient view of, 11;
    chain of, 36–37; during child-
    birth, 90; examples of, 12–14;
    explanation of, to clients, 66;
    as fall from grace, 16; as illness,
    1, 2, 11, 17, 22; indicators of,
    22–23, 202; and loss of com-
    munity, 89; caused by trauma,
    4, 11, 37, 169; viewed as psy-
    chological phenomenon, 22,
    36; voluntary, 111–12
Soul parts: existence of, in nonor-
    dinary worlds, 20–21, 23, 38;
    integration of, 69, 74, 91, 129,
    135, 163, 174; multiple, 72–74;
    welcoming home, 43, 55, 57,
    58, 75, 86, 87, 95. *See also*
    Blowing; Soul retrieval, effects
    of
Soul retrieval: applications for
    counseling, 113; as ceremony,
    68, 81–82, 85; compared
    to psychotherapy, 38–40;
    classical examples, 78–80;
    creating the space for, 68–69;
    commitment to therapy and,
    151; in other cultures, 78–82,
    85–86, 170; from the dead, 79,
    113–18; effects of, 66, 125–36,
    137–49, 155, 157–58; ethics
    in, 64, 76; life after, 87,
    161–63, 165–68, 169, 171;
    literature on, 78; need for,
    14, 170; through negotiation,
    37; nonshamanic ceremonies,
    78; readiness for, 134, 153–54,
    190–91; repeated, 170;

Vietnam veterans, 20, 91. *See also*
 Combat
Violence, 37, 90, 113
Vision, 161–62, 165
Visualizing: method of protec-
 tion, 102; in soul retrieval, 74,
 166, 178
Void, 42, 43, 44, 203; illustrated,
 43
Von Franz, Marie, 22

War. *See* Combat
Water pollution, 193–94, 195, 197
Whale, as power animal, 33
Wholeness, 11, 26–27, 143, 190,
 191
Will, role of, in shamanic jour-
 ney, 71
Wise, Anna, 29
Wounded healers, 15, 22, 202